W9-CTS-363

Navigating the Organizational Lifecycle

A Capacity-Building Guide for Nonprofit Leaders

By **Paul M. Connolly**

BOARDSOURCE®
Building Effective Nonprofit Boards

Formerly the National Center for Nonprofit Boards

strategies to achieve social impact

Library of Congress Cataloging-in-Publication Data

Connolly, Paul, 1962-

   Navigating the organizational lifecycle : a capacity-building guide for nonprofit leaders / by Paul M. Connolly.

     p. cm.

   Includes bibliographical references.

   ISBN 1-58686-087-9 (pbk.)

   1. Nonprofit organizations--Management. 2. Organizational change. 3. Organizational effectiveness. I. Title.

   HD62.6.C6637 2006
   658'.048--dc22

                                  2005024946

© 2006 BoardSource.
First printing, October 2005.
ISBN 1-58686-087-9

Published by BoardSource
1828 L Street, NW, Suite 900
Washington, DC 20036

This publication may not be reproduced without permission. Permission can be obtained by completing a request for permission form located at www.boardsource.org. Revenue from publications sales ensures the capacity of BoardSource to produce resources and provide services to strengthen the governing boards of nonprofit organizations. Copies of this book and all other BoardSource publications can be ordered by calling 800-883-6262. Discounts are available for bulk purchases.

The views in each BoardSource publication are those of its author, and do not represent official positions of BoardSource or its sponsoring organizations.

BOARDSOURCE®
Building Effective Nonprofit Boards

Formerly the National Center for Nonprofit Boards

BoardSource, formerly the National Center for Nonprofit Boards, is the premier resource for practical information, tools and best practices, training, and leadership development for board members of nonprofit organizations worldwide. Through our highly acclaimed programs and services, BoardSource enables organizations to fulfill their missions by helping build strong and effective nonprofit boards.

BoardSource provides assistance and resources to nonprofit leaders through workshops, training, and our extensive Web site, www.boardsource.org. A team of BoardSource governance consultants works directly with nonprofit leaders to design specialized solutions to meet organizations' needs and assists nongovernmental organizations around the world through partnerships and capacity building. As the world's largest, most comprehensive publisher of materials on nonprofit governance, BoardSource offers a wide selection of books, videotapes, CDs, and online tools. BoardSource also hosts the BoardSource Leadership Forum, bringing together governance experts, board members, and chief executives of nonprofit organizations from around the world.

Created out of the nonprofit sector's critical need for governance guidance and expertise, BoardSource is a 501(c)(3) nonprofit organization that has provided practical solutions to nonprofit organizations of all sizes in diverse communities. In 2001, BoardSource changed its name from the National Center for Nonprofit Boards to better reflect its mission. Today, BoardSource has approximately 8,000 members and has served more than 75,000 nonprofit leaders.

For more information, please visit our Web site, www.boardsource.org, e-mail us at mail@boardsource.org, or call us at 800-883-6262.

Have You Used These BoardSource Resources?

VIDEOS

Meeting the Challenge: An Orientation to Nonprofit Board Service

Speaking of Money: A Guide to Fundraising for Nonprofit Board Members

BOOKS

The Board Chair Handbook

Managing Conflicts of Interest: Practical Guidelines for Nonprofit Boards

Driving Strategic Planning: A Nonprofit Executive's Guide

The Board-Savvy CEO: How To Build a Strong, Positive Relationship with Your Board

Presenting: Board Orientation

Presenting: Nonprofit Financials

Meet Smarter: A Guide to Better Nonprofit Board Meetings

The Board Building Cycle: Nine Steps to Finding, Recruiting, and Engaging Nonprofit Board Members

The Policy Sampler: A Resource for Nonprofit Boards

To Go Forward, Retreat! The Board Retreat Handbook

Nonprofit Board Answer Book: Practical Guide for Board Members and Chief Executives

Nonprofit Board Answer Book II: Beyond the Basics

The Nonprofit Legal Landscape

Self-Assessment for Nonprofit Governing Boards

Assessment of the Chief Executive

Fearless Fundraising

The Nonprofit Board's Guide to Bylaws

Understanding Nonprofit Financial Statements

Transforming Board Structure: New Possibilities for Committees and Task Forces

THE GOVERNANCE SERIES

1. *Ten Basic Responsibilities of Nonprofit Boards*
2. *Financial Responsibilities of Nonprofit Boards*
3. *Structures and Practices of Nonprofit Boards*
4. *Fundraising Responsibilities of Nonprofit Boards*
5. *Legal Responsibilities of Nonprofit Boards*
6. *The Nonprofit Board's Role in Setting and Advancing the Mission*
7. *The Nonprofit Board's Role in Planning and Evaluation*
8. *How To Help Your Board Govern More and Manage Less*
9. *Leadership Roles in Nonprofit Governance*

For an up-to-date list of publications and information about current prices, membership, and other services, please call BoardSource at 800-883-6262 or visit our Web site at www.boardsource.org.

Contents

Exhibits

CD-ROM

The CD-ROM attached to the back of the book provides an electronic version of Appendix 2 for customization and distribution purposes.

Acknowledgements

My thinking about nonprofit organizational capacity and lifecycles had a long gestation period before this book was born. It is based primarily on my consulting experience with a wide range of nonprofit organizations — small and large, young and mature, across all subsectors — over the past 15 years. While working with this array of clients, I began to see patterns and typical phases and characteristics of nonprofits at each stage of their evolution.

My conceptual framework for thinking about nonprofit organizational lifecycles was inspired about 10 years ago by Sue Stevens' seminal essay, "Growing Up Nonprofit," as well as the writing on the topic by Karl Mathiasen and the Management Assistance Group (Mathiasen wrote *Board Passages: Three Key Stages in a Nonprofit Board's Lifecycle*, published by BoardSource in 1999). My framework also incorporates concepts based on the types of capacity that Christine Letts, William Ryan, and Allen Grossman described in their book, *High Performance Nonprofits: Managing Upstream for Impact.* Judith Sharken Simon's book on nonprofit lifecycles and Carl Sussman's writing on adaptive capacity also contributed greatly to my knowledge. I thank them and all those whose works I cite.

My thinking on the role of funders in supporting capacity building has been informed by my close collaboration with Carol Lukas of the Amherst Wilder Foundation, with whom I co-authored *Strengthening Nonprofit Performance: A Funder's Guide to Capacity Building.* A few parts of this book were adapted from that publication.

Recently, Gayle Williams and Sandra Mikush of the Mary Reynolds Babcock Foundation asked me to apply the organizational capacity model to each of the lifecycle stages and articulate stage-based investment strategies for funders. They also arranged a dynamic brainstorming session that included themselves, Gladys Washington, William Buster, Kathie deNobriga, and Kenneth Jones. This group's thoughts are reflected throughout this book.

I am especially appreciative of my colleagues at TCC Group who contributed to the creation of this book. John Riggan and Richard Mittenthal provided generous encouragement and support. Peter York is a true thought partner and made major contributions to the ideas in this book, especially related to the model for organizational capacity. (Peter and I developed the capacity model years ago for the David and Lucile Packard Foundation, under the very helpful direction of Barbara Kibbe and Stephanie McAuliffe.) Laura Colin Klein worked closely with me to identify traits associated with the lifecycles stages and transitions. Anne Sherman helped develop the views expressed in this book related to adaptive and leadership capacity. And Cara Cipollone, Evan Kultangwatana, Laura Meislin, Aracely Ruiz, and Andrew Smith assisted with the research for and development of this book.

I also want to acknowledge Marla Bobowick of BoardSource for encouraging me to write this book in the first place. Thanks also to George Gates and especially Claire Perella at BoardSource for their guidance during the book development process, and to Dennis Bass for editing the manuscript.

Finally, I thank my family and friends for all of their support, especially my parents, Joe and Ann Connolly.

Introduction

Of what use is a book about the life patterns of nonprofit organizations to a board of directors or a chief executive?

If there are common events and stages that all or most nonprofits experience, then the leaders of the organization who understand those patterns can benefit immensely — by helping their nonprofit anticipate, prepare for, and navigate those predictable passages and changes. In short, they will be able to do a better job of discharging their public trust as the leaders responsible for ensuring that the organization successfully achieves its non-profit mission. Especially in the current environment of increasing scrutiny of governance performance, it is essential to be aware of an organization's place in development and to be strategic in planning for the future. Nonprofits must adapt and grow, not only with their own inevitable changes, but also with those of the sector as a whole.

This book elucidates, for both senior executives and board members, a theory of the evolutionary development of nonprofit organizations, giving those leaders a rational and useful road map to guide them through what must often seem like a murky and unexplored nonprofit landscape. And, although styled as theory, it has some very practical and concrete applications.

This theory merges two concepts of the evolution of nonprofits: the lifecycle model and the capacity model. Specifically, the book explains

- The nonprofit organizational lifecycle model — and why it matters.

- The core components of organizational capacity and how they change during each lifecycle stage.

- How a board's composition and responsibilities may change at each stage of the lifecycle.

- How to assess a nonprofit organization's stage of development.

- How to anticipate future challenges, align capacities and lifecycle stages, manage organizational transitions, and strengthen capacities.

- How to obtain funder support for nonprofit organizational development.

Funders themselves will benefit from understanding the lifecycle model, how it is relevant to grant recipients, and how they can strengthen grantees through capacity-building investments. Consultants, trainers, and others who provide management and governance assistance to nonprofit organizations can learn how to apply the lifecycle and capacity models to their clients and design tailored approaches to help them strengthen their performance and navigate passages.

Chapter 1 explains the two main frameworks used to understand the life of a nonprofit: the organizational lifecycle model and the organizational capacity model. This chapter defines the developmental stages and capacities that are referred to throughout the rest of the book.

Chapter 2 integrates the two models and describes the optimal and shifting capacities necessary to move successfully through each phase of the lifecycle. The chapter includes descriptions of each lifecycle stage with normative capacities during each of those stages, enabling the reader to identify where his or her organization is in the lifecycle and the strengths and weaknesses that may need to be addressed. The chapter also discusses the transitions between stages and includes brief case studies to illustrate how specific nonprofits navigated transitions for those stages.

Chapter 3 focuses on how a nonprofit can enhance the four main types of organizational capacity and provides guidance about an array of capacity-building activities. In particular, this chapter delves into more detail about the individual components of the four core capacities, and includes tips for strengthening them in different stages of the organization's lifecycle.

If they are to implement the capacity-building recommendations made in earlier chapters, nonprofits often need help from outsiders in order to successfully make those improvements, including special funding. Chapter 4 briefly lists types of external service providers and explains how to make the case to funders for capacity-building support.

Appendix 1 of this book outlines proficiencies that were found to be common among high-performing nonprofits. It can be used as markers for each organization to strive towards. The lifecycle assessment tool in Appendix 2 can help a nonprofit's leaders assess the organization's stage of development and make a detailed diagnosis of strengths and weaknesses at that current stage. This will initiate discussion and action by organizational leaders to further capacity building and alignment. Appendix 3 provides a detailed outline for how to customize a proposal for funding to a nonprofit's current stage of development, as briefly discussed in Chapter 4.

Finally, a list of suggested resources for the reader is included in the back of the text. These resources are broken down into specific categories of capacity and stages in the lifecycle, attempting to provide more specific and applicable guidance and information that goes beyond the scope of this book.

When reading the text that follows, one may be misled into believing that every nonprofit fits neatly into the stages and the capacities that support them, or that the capacities described as desirable for a given stage in the lifecycle are ideal for every nonprofit. But, like life for humans, life for nonprofits is often messy and unpredictable. And, as for humans, diagnosing and prescribing remedies for nonprofits doesn't always follow a textbook. This book intends to help nonprofit leaders recognize their organization's situation using the tools and concepts offered here, and to take action accordingly. It is important to remember that nonprofits often find themselves in a new life stage by surprise rather than through planning or with any foresight. The following chapters encourage leadership be more proactive and informed about growth and change.

1.
What Are Nonprofit Lifecycles and Capacities?

LIFECYCLE MODEL

Since the massive expansion of the nonprofit sector in the 20th century, academics and economists have conceptualized several theories to explain change, growth, and decay in these organizations. One of the most useful theories is the lifecycle model, succinctly summarized by the noted philanthropic leader, John W. Gardner: "Like people and plants, organizations have a lifecycle. They have a green and supple youth, a time of flourishing and strengths, and a gnarled old age."[1]

Indeed, most concepts about the lifecycles of organizations spring from theories about human development. Psychologist Eric Erikson described eight life phases during which a person needs to master specific challenges: In the early stages, children need to form trusting relationships, develop physical abilities, become more independent, and learn new skills in school. During the teenage years, individuals must clarify their identities. Adults need to form intimate relationships, support the next generation, and accept themselves during the final periods of life. Erikson believed that at each turning point, people need to resolve the conflict of that stage and adapt their personalities in order to cope well and move onto the next phase.[2] Such transitions usually involve transformational change.

Nonprofit organizational development is loosely theorized to be similar to human development in that there are stages through which each nonprofit passes with foreseeable features and characteristics. Though the borders between stages are often overlapping, each nonprofit must navigate the transitions from one stage to another. These turning points are often difficult, like the growing pains of human adolescence, the lethargy of a midlife crisis, or the downward spiral of the dying process. (Of course, there are limits to the parallels between human and organizational development. For example, the human lifecycle is truly linear, culminating in death for all, while organizations have the potential to extend their existence into perpetuity.)

The basic lifecycle model outlined here encompasses five stages:

1. Start-up

2. Adolescent

3. Mature

4. Stagnant

5. Defunct

---

1. Lippit, Gordon L. and Warren Schmidt. "Crises in a Developing Organization." *Harvard Business Review*, 1967.

2. Erikson, E. H. and J. M. Erikson. *The Life-Cycle Completed: A Review.* New York: W.W. Norton, 1987.

Organizational development through these stages is an organic, nonlinear flow. To reflect this, Exhibit 1 shows the lifecycle of a nonprofit as a curve, with the possibility — at each stage — of stagnating and dissolving, or renewing and reverting to an earlier stage.[3] Traits normally associated with nonprofits at each phase are described in detail in Chapter 2.

EXHIBIT 1: THE NONPROFIT ORGANIZATIONAL LIFECYCLE MODEL

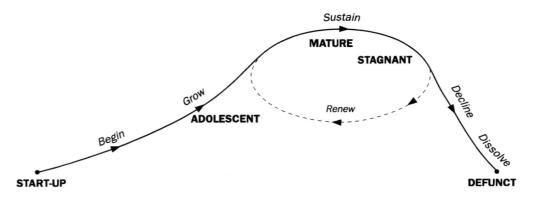

As illustrated above, after start-up a nonprofit usually, but not *always*, moves through adolescence and into maturity. When a nonprofit organization stagnates, it typically either renews itself and continues to grow, or declines into obsolescence and ultimately becomes defunct and dissolves. The transitions between stages (begin, grow, decline, renew, and dissolve), as well as the process to sustain an organization in maturity, are explained in more detail in Chapter 2.

It is important to keep in mind that this model is only a framework that shows the typical path of a nonprofit's journey. It is theoretical and not based on empirical evidence. It is not meant to be deterministic, and there are many exceptions in the real world:

- Not all nonprofit organizations go through every stage. Some start-ups do not even get off the ground, but move right to obsolescence, closing down after just a few years. A nonprofit can make dramatic leaps — forward or back — at any point during its lifecycle. Thus, sometimes the lifecycle may look more like a serpent's back than a gentle curve.

- Budget size does not necessarily correlate directly to this model, but groups with smaller budgets (under $1 million annually) tend to be in the earlier stages of the lifecycle and ones with larger budgets (over $1 million) are usually more complex and in a later stage of development. A recent survey found that more than half of the nonprofits running at less than $1 million per year were 15 years old or younger, compared with 19 percent of organizations running at $2 million to $10 million, and just 7 percent of organizations running at more than $10 million.[4] It is, of course, possible for a small group to reach maturity before a larger one — especially if the

---

3. Aspects of this model are adapted from the models described in Susan Kenny Stevens' essay, "Growing Up Nonprofit," and *Nonprofit Lifecycles: Stage-Based Wisdom for Nonprofit Capacity* (2001), as well as Karl Mathiasen and the Management Assistance Group's writings on this topic.

4. Light, Paul C. *Pathways to Nonprofit Excellence*. Washington, DC: Brookings Institution Press, 2002.

need the larger group is trying to address is a major problem in society — but smaller groups tend to be younger than larger ones. Another exception to the budget-lifecycle correlation is trade associations or other mutual-benefit groups, like some labor unions, with stable and finite audiences and clientele. For example, an association of cell-phone manufacturers, with a known and stable number of potential members, may have essentially the same size budget and serve about the same number of clients from start-up through maturity.

- The rate at which a nonprofit passes through its lifecycle also differs greatly. Consider the case of an association with a small client base: It may move through early stages of the lifecycle at a remarkably rapid pace because of its easily identifiable constituent audience and its cohesive mission. Or a healthy social-service agency may go rapidly through start-up to maturity because it receives a large infusion of early funding when demand is high and there are few alternative providers. By contrast, a community-based health clinic, operating in a setting where need is great and there are many similar providers, may have a long trajectory of adolescent growth that lasts several decades. Some organizations will never even reach full maturity before declining.

- Keep in mind that a nonprofit's ability to achieve its mission through delivery of effective programs and services is the predominant determinant of its particular lifecycle phase. The level, quality, reach, and impact of its programs and services are a better measurement of developmental stage than are its age, budget size, or number of staff. (Just consider how many older nonprofits have large budgets and staffs, but are ineffective in attaining their missions.)

Passages between lifecycle stages are often difficult and destabilizing for organizations because they require change. Sometimes groups can plan a transformation intentionally, such as when the founder of a fledgling animal-rights advocacy group announces his or her plan to leave, and the board seeks a new leader to grow the organization to the next level. At other times, however, the environment forces a transition in organizations, such as when health-care finance reforms in the 1990s required community-health clinics across the country to redesign their business models, and sometimes move or revert to a different stage in their lifecycle. To ensure a smooth transition at any point, board and senior executives can engage in candid and thoughtful assessment and deliberate strategic planning.

Appropriate strategies for one stage can often become inappropriate in the next. It is not unusual for an organization to end each phase with a crisis, upon finding that it has outgrown prior methods of behavior. For example, an entrepreneurial, visionary leader who is perfectly suited for a start-up theater troupe may not have the strong management skills that will enable the group to become a mature performing-arts center. Or the hands-on board of a new charter school, when it moves into the mature stage of an established educational institution, may be perceived by the staff to be micromanaging. Likewise, the formal hierarchy and operating systems that allow an expanding agency to mature can harden into a kind of organizational straitjacket — a rigid and outmoded structure and set of procedures that get in the way of effective operations and lead to stagnation.

One characteristic seems common to all nonprofits: **Any group that aims to deliver successfully on its mission must attain the mature stage — and sustain itself there.** Some may argue that certain small grass-roots organizations are most effective by remaining in the effervescent, "Peter Pan"–like state of perpetual childhood and by avoiding staid adulthood, but these groups are probably not fully tapping their potential. While in adolescence, a nonprofit will typically determine its ultimate mission and the right path to maturity. During maturity, the nonprofit should be confident in its aims and courses, yet retain the flexibility to make constant adjustments along the way. Mature nonprofits must be vibrant, too, in the same way that a self-aware and secure adult retains a positive, youthful perspective in old age.

Maturity is a mission-driven stage. Reaching maturity means that all of the core capacities (introduced below) of a nonprofit organization are aligned and functioning effectively to advance its mission. A fully actualized, mature organization should remain vital and increasingly improve the quality of its programs — so as to make significant progress in fulfilling the defined need for which it exists.

The lifecycle model is one tool that nonprofit board members and chief executives can use to assess their organization and gain a better understanding of where it is today, where it may be lagging, and where it is going in the future. The lifecycle model can help anticipate problems and provide strategies to enhance the organization's effectiveness. Additionally, it can reveal how unexplained internal tensions or mission failures may occur due to the challenges of a transition between stages. But, is the lifecycle model a comprehensive explanation of nonprofit organizational development? Or are there other factors, such as an organization's capabilities and capacities that can add to our understanding?

CAPACITY MODEL

In *Adaptation to Life*, a study of the mental health of a group of people over a 35-year period, George E. Vaillant discovered that the differences in individuals' adaptive mechanisms can explain why some people manage to cope effectively with various stages and transitions in their lives, while others cope badly or not at all. As Vaillant notes, "a broken love affair may lead one man to write great poetry and another to commit suicide."[5] It is the ability to learn — especially from past experience — to be reflective, flexible, and adaptable that determines whether life's conflicts can be mastered. The non-profit capacity model is premised on the theory that similar capacities are also essential to the health of nonprofit organizations.

Capacity is an abstract term that describes a wide range of capabilities, knowledge, and resources that nonprofits need in order to be vital and effective in staying true to their mission. Like an individual's mental health, organizational capacity is multifaceted and continually evolving. A nonprofit's capacity develops as the organization advances and enables it to manage transitions at critical turning points. An entire system of interrelated parts — including programs, governance, financial management, fund development, and human resources — need to be present. The various elements of capacity influence not only the organization's ability to achieve mission, but other elements of organizational capacity as well. Additionally, the organization needs to have the ability to adapt those parts, altering the mix and level of capacities that are necessary at each stage and ensuring that all parts work together, for the nonprofit to move through its lifecycle and achieve its mission. Adaptation and capacity development are the hallmarks of successful nonprofit organizations that deliver quality programs and fulfill the needs of society.

---

5. Vaillant, George E. *Adaptation to Life*. Boston, MA: Little Brown and Company, 1977.

Exhibit 2 illustrates a model for understanding nonprofit organizational capacity.[6] The four core components of the model are *adaptive capacity, leadership capacity, management capacity*, and *technical capacity*. These capacities will typically undergo transformations during the various phases of the lifecycle, if a nonprofit is to transition successfully from one stage to another. An organization's culture, resources, and external environment influence its capacity, as indicated in the center and outer rings of Exhibit 2.

EXHIBIT 2: THE NONPROFIT ORGANIZATIONAL CAPACITY MODEL

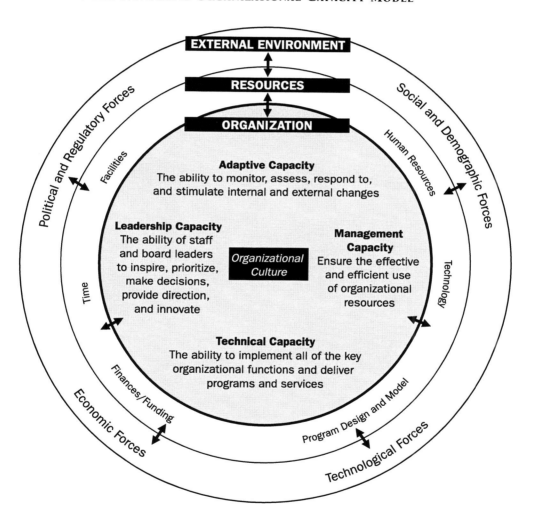

---

6. This model was initially presented in a June 2003 report by TCC Group, *Building the Capacity of Capacity Builders*, which was prepared with support from the David and Lucile Packard Foundation. TCC Group based this model on a synthesis of the perspectives of many researchers and leaders in the nonprofit and governance field who have put forth definitions of nonprofit organizational effectiveness.

In developing the necessary capacities, leaders are staying on a more direct path to monitoring, maintaining, and strengthening organizational performance. Let's briefly explore how this model relates to organizational growth and progress:

Adaptive capacity is the ability to monitor, assess, respond to, and stimulate internal and external changes. Although it may be the least familiar term of the four capacities, it is probably the most important capacity because it enables a nonprofit to be innovative, flexible, and resilient. It entails being constantly attuned to the external environment in order to identify changes and opportunities, to generate new ideas, and to modify or initiate strategies in response to the changes, opportunities, and ideas. Adaptive nonprofits are inquisitive and act as learning organizations, which Peter Senge describes as when entities "continually expand their capacity to create the results they truly desire, where new and expansive patterns of thinking are nurtured, where collective aspiration is set free, and where people are continually learning to see the whole together."[7] By always learning and improving, a nonprofit is able to use its existing resources more effectively and efficiently and to acquire new resources in a more intentional and mission-focused way. Also note that adaptive capacity is not just about being reactive; it requires being proactive and generative by playing an advocacy role to shape the external environment in which the organization operates. A nonprofit can strengthen its adaptive capacity by conducting periodic needs assessments, organizational assessments, and program evaluations; engaging in knowledge management and planning; and pursuing collaborations and partnerships.

Leadership capacity is the ability of all organizational leaders — both senior executives and board members — to inspire, prioritize, make decisions, provide direction, and innovate in a concerted effort to achieve the organizational mission. Leadership capacity is also important because leaders must make effective and strategic decisions based on what they learn through the activities that enhance adaptive capacity. If an organization is poorly led, it is unlikely that it will be able to manage its work well over the long term. Leadership capacity can be enhanced through board development, executive leadership development, and leadership transitions.

Management capacity is the ability of a nonprofit to ensure the effective and efficient use of organizational resources — human and financial. It involves hiring, training, and assessing staff, as well as providing them with incentives and resources to perform well. It includes creating an organizational structure, solving internal problems, and facilitating clear communications among staff. It also entails using financial information to inform organizational decisions and managing financial resources with accountability to ensure that they are effectively and efficiently supporting the organization's mission. Management capacity can be improved through human resource development and management, internal communications, and financial management.

Technical capacity is the ability to perform key operational functions and deliver programs and services. Essentially, it is the capability of staff members to do the work of the organization. There are mixed views about the extent of nonprofit organizations' technical capacity. On one hand, some believe that nonprofits are especially strong in this area since the artists, social workers, teachers, lawyers, and others who work for nonprofits are usually passionate about and skilled in the services they offer. On the other hand,

---

7. Senge, Peter M. *The Fifth Discipline: The Art and Practice of the Learning Organizations*. New York: Doubleday Currently, 1990.

some skeptics feel that nonprofits often do not deliver programs and services effectively, indicating weakness in technical capacity. In any case, technical capacity is built by substantive professional development of the program staff; increasing their skills in service delivery, evaluation, outreach, and advocacy; building staff capacity in marketing communications, fundraising, and earned-income generation; and improving accounting, legal, facilities management, and technological skills.

INTERRELATIONSHIP OF THE FOUR CORE CAPACITIES

How do the adaptive, leadership, management, and technical capacities relate to each other? To understand this, it's helpful to know a bit more about how nonprofits typically utilize core capacities:

- Adaptive capacity is most often the leading element in a nonprofit's evolution. During the start-up and adolescent stages, a nonprofit builds its adaptive capacity by learning about its abilities and the outside world, trying new things, and learning from its experiments along the way. A mature nonprofit is self-reflective and continually makes adjustments to stay vibrant and achieve its mission. Stagnant and defunct nonprofits have essentially lost their adaptive capacity.

- Leadership capacity and adaptive capacity are interdependent. To do well, leaders need knowledge about the organization and its external environment. They are also responsible for many of the activities that improve adaptive capacity, such as organizational assessment, program evaluation, and strategic planning and thinking. If adaptive and leadership capacities are not well aligned, an organization faces a major challenge.

- Management capacity is usually heavily dependent on leadership capacity since leaders direct the management function of an organization. If leaders provide poor guidance to internal staff and make unwise decisions, management capacity will be compromised.

- Technical capacity is typically more independent from the other three capacities. If an organization knows what it needs to accomplish but has trouble performing and delivering, this displays poor technical capacity, even when other capacities may be robust. Conversely, if the other capacities are weak but technical capacity is vigorous, an organization may implement programs and activities well, but they may be the wrong things for the organization to do in order to achieve its mission.

Ideally, an organization should strive to have its four core capabilities in alignment, i.e., each capacity at or near the strength appropriate to its lifecycle stage. Why? If the core capacities are aligned in an organization, they will reinforce each other and enhance the organization's ability to deliver programs and services — thereby enabling the group to achieve its mission.

Think of it as the core abilities that allow one to drive a car in order to reach a chosen destination: Leadership capacity is the driver's ability to determine where he wants to go and to set a course to get there. Adaptive capacity is his proficiency in making adjustments — and even changing direction — when weather, traffic, or fuel availability shift. Management capacity is the driver's ability to address problems as they arise, such as running low on gas or getting a flat tire. Finally, technical capacity is the driver being licensed and knowing the rules of the road, as well as having some mechanical skills necessary to diagnose and repair a vehicle competently. If these four capacities are in general alignment, they will complement each other and enable the driver to reach his destination.

Exhibit 3 below shows a conceptual mapping of the difference between a loosely and a tightly aligned set of capacities. When capacities are tightly aligned, the organization is more centered, grounded, and works under an overall strategic culture, overlapping all capacities in order to remain in proper alignment and to perform well.

EXHIBIT 3: ALIGNMENT OF CORE CAPACITIES

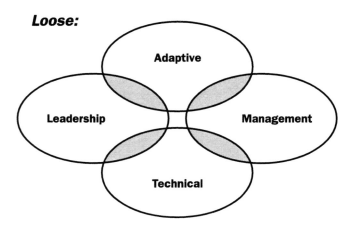

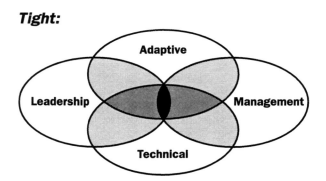

However, in the real world, all four core capacities may not evolve to the same level and at the same rate. As shown in Exhibit 4 on the next page, for most nonprofits, the usual path for capacities is for adaptive capacity to be built first, then leadership capacity. Next, management capacity is developed, which then leads to strengthening adaptive capacity to support leadership, and technical capacity to deliver program and services.[8]

Adaptive and leadership capacities often progress ahead of others in the start-up stage because the first step for an organization is usually to comprehend what the social need is and how to design and deliver responsive programs to meet that need. Based on this, the board and senior staff make resource decisions to ensure that the management and

---

8. This framework, which is shown here and throughout Chapter 2, was developed by TCC Group's Peter York as part of an organizational effectiveness tool created in 2005 for New Hampshire's Statewide Collaborative for Enhancing Nonprofit Effectiveness.

technical capacities are in place in order to get the programs up and running. Once the capacities have been built to begin the work of the organization, board and executive leaders may then focus on strengthening adaptive capacity to get ready for the next stage (adolescence) and on shifting resources toward developing the management and technical capacities required for growth in the adolescent stage. This iterative process continues as the nonprofit evolves through subsequent phases.

EXHIBIT 4: BUILDING CAPACITIES TO EFFECTIVELY DELIVER PROGRAMS

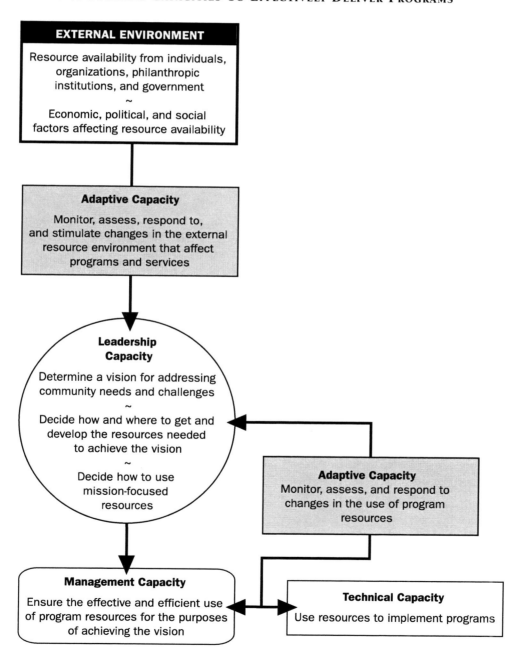

In Chapter 2, this mission-focused, capacity-building process is illustrated for each transition in a nonprofit's lifecycle — beginning, growing, sustaining, and renewing.

ORGANIZATIONAL CULTURE

The capacity-model chart (Exhibit 2) shows that *organizational culture* — the unique history, language, rituals, values, and beliefs of each nonprofit — also greatly influences each of the four core capacities. Ultimately, culture serves as the context within which an organization defines, assesses, and improves its capabilities. The manner in which organizational culture expresses itself is distinctive for each group and changes over time. However, the functions that culture plays in an organization are shared across nonprofits. Specifically, a healthy organizational culture meets three critical needs of an organization:

1. *Unify*: The organizational culture engenders open and honest communication across all levels in the organization, leading to a sense of a cohesive "group identity."

2. *Validate*: It supports and celebrates the successes of individual staff and of the organization as a whole.

3. *Energize*: It allows and encourages staff and board members to reflect on their work, to socialize, and to reconnect with their original motivations to become involved in the work.

If these needs aren't met through the culture of the organization, the nonprofit will struggle to adapt and survive.

RESOURCES

Nonprofits also rely on certain critical *resources* that directly support and affect the quality of programs and services (see second ring of Exhibit 2). Without those resources, an organization — whether an advocacy group, membership-based trade association, theater, after-school program, or university — cannot function. Key organizational resources are those that directly support program implementation and include the skills, knowledge, and experience of those delivering the services, as well as the resources provided directly to clients, such as financial assistance, in-kind resources, or equipment.

Growing a nonprofit's capacities and finding the resources necessary to support them is a bit like the chicken-or-egg question. Either can probably come first, but after the initial start, growth in capacity necessitates securing resources to support that growth. Ideally, an organization's resources and capacities grow in tandem, for if one far exceeds the other, there will be serious dislocations for the nonprofit.

Nonprofits also need to have at their disposal resources that are not directly related to service delivery, such as human resources for supporting the programmatic work of the organization, technology, program-support materials, facilities, equipment, vehicles, and supplies. An organization's level of resources at a given point in time will greatly affect how adaptive, leadership, management, and technical capacities can manifest themselves. For instance, financial resources are central to supporting each core capacity: Part of an organization's adaptive capacity is the ability to identify opportunities and challenges in the funding environment of the organization. Its management capacity is centrally concerned with making efficient and effective use of those funding resources. Financial assets and stability affect the ability of the organization to support and expand its technical capacities.

EXTERNAL ENVIRONMENT

The outer ring of Exhibit 2 illustrates that the *external environment* also greatly influences the capacities of a nonprofit — whether it's a community-development, health care, cultural, or educational organization. Social and economic trends can cause shifts in constituent needs and demands. Changes in government policy and the economy can affect the availability of funding and the pool of qualified professionals available for a nonprofit to hire.

For example: Rapid technological progress in the 1990s forced many nonprofits to automate, streamline operations, and take advantage of more affordable and efficient telecommunications. But often it was the larger, well-financed nonprofits that had the resources to do this, while many smaller nonprofits — often serving the most pressing social needs — were not able to do so. A vigilant nonprofit is constantly scanning its external environment in order to stay abreast of the social, economic, technological, and industry trends that can critically affect the organization's capacities.

Which specific capacities (beyond the four core capacities) does a nonprofit need in order to achieve its mission? Although research is in the early stages, some assessments have been done to identify organizational proficiencies that high-performing nonprofits have in common. As detailed in the following chapters, these indicators include such factors as how well the organization learns, collaborates with constituents, assesses the needs of the organization's clients, makes decisions, holds executive staff accountable, financially sustains the nonprofit, supports staff and volunteers, and develops the staff members' skills necessary to get their work done well. (See Appendix 1 for a list of indicators for high-performing organizations, and Appendix 2 for a detailed list of performance assessment questions to make that determination for your own organization.)

QUESTIONS FOR THE BOARD AND CHIEF EXECUTIVE

1. At first glance, do you recognize your own organization in one of the lifecycle stages? If so, which one and why?

2. How has your organization advanced through its lifecycle to date? How would you describe the rate of this evolution and the reason for that pace?

3. At first glance, how strong is each of your nonprofit's core capacities (adaptive, leadership, management, and technical)? In particular, how does your organization rate when you review the list of performance indicators for high-performing organizations (found in Appendix 1 on page 69)?

4. How would you describe the culture of your organization and, specifically, how unifying, validating, and re-energizing is it?

2.
Organizational Capacity and Lifecycles: How and When Do They Interrelate?

The two models explained in Chapter 1 are useful methods employed by nonprofit leaders to understand the life span of a nonprofit organization. But, it is even more important to understand the *relationship* of these two models and how they might be combined. This relationship illustrates the challenges nonprofit boards and chief executives will encounter, and how best they can meet those challenges throughout the duration of an organization's existence.

This chapter integrates the lifecycle model and the capacity model by explaining how the core capacities (adaptive, leadership, management, and technical) evolve and change through each typical stage of the lifecycle (start-up, adolescent, mature, stagnant, and defunct). At each phase, proficiencies and common characteristics are described, which indicate healthy capacity for an organization at that stage.

An important point to remember is that **the distinctions between the stages of development are often blurred and it is not unusual for an organization to exhibit capacities appropriate to different lifecycle stages at the same time.** For example, an organization may have outstanding leaders and implement programs well, exhibiting leadership and technical capacity appropriate to an adolescent nonprofit. Yet, contemporaneously, the group can have adaptive and management characteristics that look more like a typical start-up, as shown in the chart below. In this case, the organization might want to focus more on strengthening its management and adaptive capacities by improving program evaluation, strategic planning, and financial management.

EXHIBIT 5: SAMPLE SELF-ASSESSMENT SUMMARY FOR A GROWING ORGANIZATION

	Start-Up	Adolescent	Mature	Stagnant	Defunct
Adaptive Capacity	✓				
Leadership Capacity		✓			
Management Capacity	✓				
Technical Capacity		✓			

Such discrepancies are common and typically indicate that an organization is moving through a transformation from one stage to another. But if capacities become too divergent — if, for example, leadership capacity spurts ahead to the mature stage but adaptive and management capacities remain in the start-up stage — then an organization will confront serious dislocations and impair its ability to achieve its mission. In this case, it may have to take proactive steps to achieve a better alignment. This challenge requires the organization's leaders not only to focus on catching up the underdeveloped capacities, but to balance the pressure to continue focusing on growing the already-developed capacities.

Board members and chief executives reading through this chapter should keep their own organization in mind and try to identify the stages and capacities that most closely typify their nonprofit. At the end of the book, the lifecycle assessment tool in Appendix 2 can be used to conduct a more thorough diagnosis and to identify areas for improvement. Equipped with this knowledge, the root causes of organizational tensions, the alignment (or misalignment) of various organizational capacities, and potential outcomes in the future can be extrapolated. In particular, the self-assessment tool can help pinpoint the specific types of capacity that an organization needs to cultivate and improve.

START-UP

START-UP

A nonprofit is usually conceived when one or more people see a need, formulate an idea to address it, and decide to form an organization — whether it be a safe house for battered women, a neighborhood garden club, or a specialized museum — to do the necessary work. Most commonly, a new nonprofit's start-up phase lasts a few years and its annual operating budget is small (under about $250,000) but growing during this period.

The founder or group of founders is usually visionary, has a passionate commitment to the mission, and brings a high level of energy to initiating the first simple programs. If there is a single founder, this person usually acts as staff leader and assembles a small group of enthusiastic volunteers who follow and encourage the founder. If more than one person initiates the organization, they may serve as the core of the board. Initially, most start-ups operate as all-volunteer organizations (AVOs), meaning that there are no paid staff or managers and board members manage volunteers, handling all other duties themselves.

All-Volunteer Organizations

Most nonprofits begin as all-volunteer organizations (AVOs) and many — such as mutual-benefit associations, sports leagues, hobby groups, literary societies, groups sponsoring civic events — remain all-volunteer throughout their entire existences. Some other AVOs, such as supporting organizations whose main function is fundraising ("friends of" groups), may be more formalized or provide some minimal reimbursement for expenses or work, but essentially they retain an AVO structure.

Nevertheless, AVOs, which number into the hundreds of thousands of groups in the United States, go through the same lifecycle and have capacity issues similar to nonprofits that hire professional staff and managers. The main difference is that the board or core group of an AVO has not only the traditional governance and strategic planning duties of a board, but also bears direct managerial and operational responsibilities that are borne by paid staff in non-AVO nonprofits. It is essential that volunteers understand in which mode (board or staff) they are acting at any given time. As a board member, the volunteer is without individual powers but is contributing to collective decision making. When acting in a staff capacity, a volunteer works to implement decisions of the board and is accountable to the volunteer board in the same way a paid staff member would be.

Often the sections and chapters below will refer to the responsibilities and duties of the board and chief executive or senior staff at different lifecycle stages as being separate and discrete from each other. For AVOs, however, that will not be the case. Board members of an AVO, because of their managerial responsibilities, will also want to pay attention to the parts of the text that refer to chief executive or senior staff, since they will also be responsible for those tasks.

Role of the Board: An All-Encompassing Task

Typically, the board of a start-up organization plays a hands-on role in oversight and management. During this early period, an organization is particularly vulnerable, so the leaders need to be persistent, flexible, and resilient to allow programs to take root and begin to blossom.

A start-up organization's board tends to be small, homogenous, and loosely formed. As stated above, it frequently includes program volunteers. Board members usually share similar values and have a strong emotional commitment to the organization's mission. For instance, parents who serve on the board of a new school for children with learning disabilities will care deeply about the school's success. The board helps to define the organization's vision and to educate the community about the new organization. When there are no or few paid staff members, the board may also perform such hands-on operating tasks as accounting and data entry. As the size of staff increases, the board and staff leaders need to clearly articulate who will be performing which tasks in order to minimize confusion or tension.

Board members of a start-up are typically expected to bring some resources to the table — either time, money, or both. Even more, they need to tap their personal networks to secure additional resources to help build capacity. At this early stage, the board acts as a committee of the whole, rather than forming independent committees to oversee particular areas. As needs arise, board members can help to recruit others to board service.

BOARD MEMBERS OF A START-UP NONPROFIT

The qualities needed in board members of a start-up nonprofit are quite different from those of an established and long-functioning board, where directors may serve more specialized needs. Directors of a new organization, especially when the board is a small one, will need a wide range of qualities, such as

- a firm commitment to the nonprofit's mission

- time to devote to both operational and governance tasks

- energy to seek needed resources

- hands-on skills in fundraising, marketing, legal issues, financial management, technology, or industry-related matters

- inventiveness, flexibility, and optimism to persevere with limited resources

- basic knowledge of nonprofit governance

- leadership qualities

- ability to work in a team setting

BUILDING CAPACITY: ONLY THE BEGINNING

Board members and, if in existence, staff leaders benefit from meeting occasionally to reflect on how the organization is progressing and to make future plans. This effort demonstrates the necessary strengthening of adaptive capacity if a fledgling group is to advance to the next stage of its lifecycle. To assess the organization overall and its programs specifically, leaders can have periodic reflective conversations about how the nonprofit group is performing and what appears to be working with the current programs — and why. At this stage, activities for strengthening adaptive capacity can be very informal.

For needs assessment, there are hands-on ways to identify constituent needs, such as talking extensively to the nonprofit's network of community leaders and potential clients. The group also needs to have simple systems for storing, organizing, disseminating, and using its knowledge. A basic planning process may result in just a short strategic "think" piece with a two-year horizon that explains how the organization will begin and then expand. Meanwhile, the start-up would be informally cooperating with other groups, such as by sharing information and making cross-referrals.

Leadership capacity in the start-up phase is initially fostered by the founding volunteers or by the board's hire of a staff leader. The staff executive in a start-up organization is typically charismatic, adept at establishing an organization, and entrepreneurial in nature. He or she focuses on articulating the vision, developing a clear business plan, and mobilizing staff and volunteers to do the work. This person leads the design and initial implementation of the programs, as well as needs assessment and outreach. The staff leader will also want to acquire resources to support the programs through community outreach and networking, fundraising, and perhaps board member recruitment. He or she may have to juggle many tasks simultaneously and be very flexible.

Organizational structure and management systems in the start-up are informal. There are few operational routines or systems in place, little or no hierarchy, and frequent casual communications among staff and volunteers. Leaders of a start-up cultivate management capacity by gradually creating simple ways to manage human and financial resources. The nonprofit often has a small number of volunteers or staff members who are organized loosely. There are usually few or no detailed personnel policies. Staff members meet informally at places like the lunch table. Likewise, the group moves to procure sufficient human resources, such as a part-time bookkeeper, to handle the financial management function.

The technical capacity of a healthy, emerging nonprofit is fostered by developing an array of basic skills. First and foremost, the nonprofit needs fundamental capacities to deliver and evaluate simple programs. Staff members normally are versatile and perform both program and management functions. Employees of a small concert hall, for example, may help manage the stage, set up props, sell tickets, and serve as ushers.

The healthy start-up also has adequate technical ability to market its programs and services and communicate about its activities through word-of-mouth and written program descriptions. It must obtain the legal capacity necessary to create bylaws and articles of incorporation and obtain tax-exempt status so that the group can formally commence the start-up phase by incorporating as a nonprofit organization. In addition, it has accounting and financial management skills needed to set up payroll if it is compensating staff, create and manage an annual budget, establish and implement a simple accounting system, and produce annual financial statements that are audited internally and approved by the board. Finally, a robust start-up has elementary competencies to manage, operate, and maintain its facilities and internal technology.

LEGAL STEPS FOR THE START-UP NONPROFIT

There are a number of practical legal actions necessary to turn a founders' vision into a functioning reality. Among them are the following:

- Incorporating the nonprofit organization by filing articles of incorporation with the office of the secretary of state

- Drafting bylaws required for a board of directors to function

- Filing Form 1023 (or 1024 for noncharities) with the IRS to apply for the recognition of federal tax-exempt status

- Filing for state and local tax exemptions: income, property, sales tax

- Applying to the IRS for a federal Employee Identification Number (EIN) with Form SS-4

- Registering in each state where the organization plans to raise funds or do business

- Applying to the U.S. Postal Service for a nonprofit mailing permit to be eligible for lower postal rates

- Convening the first board meeting to elect officers and grant them the authority to act on behalf of the organization (executing contracts, opening bank accounts, and so forth)

The ability to procure funding is also a key technical requirement for a start-up. Board and staff leadership need to develop a basic plan for generating revenues and a simple process for budgeting to ensure that the financial resources are allocated in a responsible manner. During its infancy, a nonprofit focuses on enlisting supporters and marshalling financial resources through individual solicitation and membership fees. At the outset, funding is usually limited to one or two main sources and the organization's budget is small (usually less than $250,000).

STRIVING FOR ADOLESCENCE

Common problems that arise during the start-up phase — and which must be addressed prior to entering the adolescent stage — are difficulties meeting program demand, staff burnout, inadequate funding, and lack of sufficient systems. The key to successfully moving past the start-up phase is developing basic capabilities to design and deliver programs. This is accomplished first by building adaptive and leadership capacities, then developing initial management and technical strengths. A nonprofit is ready for the adolescent stage when it is effectively delivering the right quantity of core programs and positive word-of-mouth has begun. Exhibit 6 on the following page illustrates this progression.

Exhibit 6: Start-Up Phase: Building Capacities To Effectively Deliver Programs

✓ **Check off the capacity-building activities and transitional milestones your nonprofit has accomplished**

Mission-Based Focus: design and implementation of core program(s)
Goal: to understand what it takes to deliver the *assumed* right *quantity* of programs and services (i.e., amount, frequency, and intensity of programs)

Adaptive Capacity
- ☐ Conduct community needs assessment
- ☐ Tap existing networks to identify start-up resources
- ☐ Begin identifying and developing relationships with those who can provide programmatic start-up resources (money, time, expertise, other)

Leadership Capacity
- ☐ Articulate a vision for addressing community needs and challenges
- ☐ Decide how and where to get and develop the resources necessary for getting programs off the ground
- ☐ Decide the core elements of the programs and services

Adaptive Capacity
- ☐ Begin tracking and gathering anecdotal evidence of the types of resources it actually takes to implement programs
- ☐ Begin gathering anecdotal evidence of client satisfaction

Management Capacity
- ☐ Recruit program implementers based on interest and basic skills
- ☐ Provide general and informal feedback to program implementers
- ☐ Provide resources for program implementation

Technical Capacity
- ☐ Core programs/services begin to be provided to a small group of clients

Transitional Milestone
- ☐ Program staff/volunteers are effectively delivering core programs with respect to quantity (amount, frequency, and intensity)
- ☐ Positive "word-of-mouth" among the target population has begun

Next Step: Adolescent...

The following case study is an example of an organization's transition from the start-up phase to the adolescent.

CASE STUDY: BEGINNING LEEWAY

The start-up period for Leeway, Inc., a group that runs a nursing home in New Haven, Connecticut for people with HIV/AIDS, took several years. The organization successfully advanced through this extended infancy by having a visionary and passionate leader, attracting a wide array of supporters, and creating a solid business plan. Leeway, Inc. exhibited many characteristics common to a nonprofit start-up, including an entrepreneurial founder who perceived a problem and created an organization to address it.

In 1987, Catherine Kennedy first conceived of the organization that became Leeway. Frustrated in her job at a large insurance company in Hartford, Catherine yearned to do more socially meaningful work and began investigating voluntary opportunities to help people with AIDS. AIDS was then a burgeoning health crisis in New Haven and there were no promising treatments on the horizon. Catherine soon discovered that the only type of care available for people with AIDS in the area was in an acute-care setting at Yale-New Haven Hospital. She realized that a nursing-home model could offer care that was not only less expensive, but also more appropriate for many individuals.

Catherine then began forming relationships with leaders of community organizations that served people with AIDS. These leaders informed her about the need for services and encouraged her plans. She also enlisted the hospital, which was losing money on AIDS clients and wanted to refer them to a more suitable alternative-care facility. Meanwhile, Catherine gradually won over the local and state government officials who would need to authorize the facility and approve access to financing. By the end of 1987, she was able to establish a board of directors representing key stakeholders in the community. Catherine named the organization Leeway, meaning a shelter from harsh wind.[9]

In 1988, Catherine created an initial business plan that focused on the pressing need for a 28-bed skilled-nursing and intermediate-care facility. It included a detailed description of the wide range of services the organization would offer, as well as a staffing plan. She developed a multiyear budget to accompany the plan that projected over $1 million in operating expenses. She also took time to widely disseminate the plan and to incorporate changes and improvements suggested by others.

After several years of promoting and publicizing the plan, she and the board secured the financial support and regulatory approvals to enable Leeway to finally open its doors to patients. It has since provided medical care to more than 500 people living with HIV/AIDS. Demand for services has increased because HIV infection rates have risen in New Haven and new drug therapies have enabled people to live longer with AIDS. To respond to that growing need, Leeway opened a 10-bed extension in 2000.

Catherine Kennedy did not live to see her dream fully realized. But her legacy lives on in the vital organization that she founded. Leeway's annual operating budget has climbed to almost $5 million. And it remains Connecticut's only nursing home dedicated solely to people with HIV/AIDS.[10]

Leeway's genesis was protracted, but the organization's leaders needed the time to lay the groundwork for the organization's growth and to evolve a sound business plan. Because the founder cultivated a broad set of allies and a strong leadership team, its leaders were capable of adapting and surviving without her. Leeway was confidently able to expand into the next stage of the lifecycle.

---

9. Oster, Sharon. *Strategic Management for Nonprofit Organizations: Theory and Cases.* New York: Oxford University Press, 1995.

10. Livingston, Catherine. "AIDS Activists in New Haven Raise Awareness." *Yale Daily News.* October 2, 2003. http://www.yaledailynews.com/article.asp?AID=23387.

ADOLESCENT

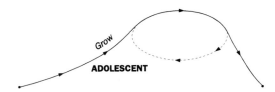

Nonprofit adolescence is often accompanied by uncertainty and angst, in the same way that teenagers often go through a bumpy period of growing pains. Although age and size can vary widely, this stage often occurs between the third and sixth year of an organization's existence, during which time its annual operating budget grows from approximately $250,000 to about one or two million dollars.

For nonprofits, this phase normally entails expansion of new programs, broader outreach, more staff, and larger quarters. Frequently, the adolescent nonprofit experiences instability when it does not adequately anticipate the systems required to support this growth. Consider the generation of AIDS/HIV organizations that were born during the onset of the AIDS crisis in the mid- and late-1980s, as illustrated in the story of Leeway. While demand exploded during the first half of the 1990s, many of these organizations went through turbulent periods because they did not foresee the changes in management, infrastructure, and fundraising that were needed to extend their services.

ROLE OF THE BOARD: MOVING FROM HANDS-ON TO OVERSIGHT

During expansion, the chief executive and board focus on meeting early programmatic goals for quantity of clients served and quality of services. They will also want to undertake a formal self-assessment process to be sure all board members are clear about their roles and responsibilities, articulate a clear theory of change, develop simple systems for gathering and using data about programmatic outcomes, and incorporate all of this valuable information into a strategic planning process. The strategic plan will typically lay out clear goals and have a 3-5 year horizon. Following the formation of a strategic plan, annual objectives for an operational plan can be adopted. Strategic planning gives a nonprofit an opportunity to readjust its priorities and programs and create a realistic blueprint for the midterm future. The planning process itself can have a galvanizing effect on teamwork, staff commitment, morale, and overall momentum.

To adapt and stay relevant, the board and chief executive of an adolescent organization need to monitor the group's progress and relate it to developments in the outside world that could influence its effectiveness and viability. Leaders of an organization in the adolescent phase will want to look ahead to ascertain the appropriate structure and basic functioning framework for their nonprofit. This is an opportune time for a group to undertake deliberate needs assessment and program evaluation, and to establish a more formal system for documenting and managing its knowledge. Market research can enable an organization to take stock of the demand for current or potential services and to tailor programs to meet changing needs. By deepening and broadening connections with constituents and evaluating its programs in simple ways, a nonprofit can keep its pulse on how needs are shifting and the programs are working — or not working.

How To Structure a Needs Assessment

Before launching an extensive program or campaign, a prudent organization conducts a needs assessment. The purpose is to determine whether the idea has merit and if it is reasonable to expect that the plan will succeed. The key components of a needs assessment are

- Identifying the target population that would benefit from the planned activity or that would be the object to provide support for an activity (e.g., abused women for a women's shelter or donors for a capital campaign)

- Classifying already available services, products, or other resources available for the target group

- Analyzing possible missing links, gaps, or lost opportunities that would open the door for the planned activity

- Defining the needed steps for launching a successful activity

If the plan gets a green light after this broad study, a more comprehensive and detailed survey would focus on strategic timing, budget, type of people, and other key elements needed to carry out the activity to a successful completion.

As the nonprofit organization matures into adolescence, the board typically expands and develops a deeper sense of organizational ownership. It may also formalize its structure by creating a few committees to oversee such critical areas as fundraising, financial oversight, or board recruitment. Board membership gradually shifts from hands-on volunteers to specialists and professionals since their main interests will no longer be the applied work. Thus, some board members may leave during this transition. As staff expands and takes on more responsibility for day-to-day tasks, the board will need to relinquish its operational role and focus more on advice, oversight, and long-term planning. Although gradually forgoing any daily direct involvement, board members still have a strong role to play in ensuring that programs are being implemented well, that evaluation efforts are being made, and that the community at large is being informed about the programs' strengths.

STRENGTHENING CAPACITY: TAKING IT A STEP FURTHER

In the adolescent phase, activities for enhancing adaptive capacity usually become more formalized. Sound adolescent organizations develop wider and deeper relationships with community leaders, funders, and constituents, and learn about needs through these interactions and through deliberate market research. The chief executive will want to continually assess and refine the programs and persuade the community and donors of their value. In addition, he or she usually establishes a professional network by developing long-term relationships with important community leaders and stakeholders who can support the organization. The chief executive of a growing community-development corporation, for example, will want to meet with local politicians, housing advocates, United Way officials, and bank officers.

Leadership capacity in the adolescent organization ought to be consciously cultivated at the executive and board level. Usually, the board increases its size, formalizes its role, and writes job descriptions for its members. Board and staff roles should be defined and separated, encouraging the board to let go of managerial tasks and focus on oversight and strategy. During this process, the chief executive's role is differentiated from the board's role. The executive now will be expected to manage the organization while segregating personal from organizational needs. Succession plans are usually drawn up for both staff and board leadership.

The board's role in financial management becomes more sophisticated as well. Organizational leaders will want to move toward multiyear budgets and will implement systems for projecting the future financially, as well as strategically. This, along with technical improvements discussed below, will enable board members to regularly analyze financial data to inform their decision making on allocating financial resources, managing cash flow, and keeping income and expenses in balance. The board of a growing nonprofit should be sensitive to any budgetary need to pare expenses by dropping or curtailing nonessential or noncore services. Board members also become more accountable for meeting fundraising targets by contributing personal donations and by soliciting funds to support programmatic growth and general operations.

The healthy nonprofit also seeks methodically to strengthen its technical capacity during adolescence. The organization's leaders will want to improve its technical capacity to provide accurate financial information by implementing an accrual accounting system and creating quarterly financial reports. It is necessary to produce an annual financial statement that is audited by an outside Certified Public Accountant. Likewise, the fit nonprofit obtains the legal capacity to handle more complicated issues related to employment, leases, and insurance.

A nonprofit at this stage typically can no longer rely on word-of-mouth to attract clients and supporters to its programs. It will need to develop basic communication methods to get the word out to potential constituents — whether they are gallery visitors, association members, synagogue worshipers, or immigrant adults who want to learn English as a second language. The organization markets its programs and services and communicates about its activities in simple ways, such as creating an extensive organizational brochure. A basic Web site can also be created and maintained.

As mentioned above, a growing nonprofit professionalizes and diversifies its technical capacities in fundraising and earned-income activities in order to generate more revenue to support its anticipated expansion. Fundraising efforts might include a more sophisticated or targeted approach to individuals, foundations, and corporations. Earned-income strategies might include developing fee-based services or starting a nonprofit business venture, such as selling greeting cards to support international relief efforts or establishing a catering business to employ and train economically disadvantaged people. Membership associations may want to consider tiered pricing strategies for membership fees.

Lastly, the adolescent nonprofit now develops technical skills to manage, operate, and maintain its internal technology and facilities, such as leasing and maintaining additional space for expanding programs. During this period, a nonprofit formalizes and systematizes operations and strengthens its infrastructure with, for example, computer systems that are necessary to support programs. However, program upgrades, enhanced computer systems, and larger facilities may require sizable investments, so the board and chief executive must balance those considerations — and be reasonably certain that the requisite funding or earned income will be available. To keep its edge on technology and facilities, no organization should take a fiscal leap that jeopardizes its operations or very survival.

CLIMBING TOWARDS THE TOP

Unfortunately, many nonprofits beyond a few years old tend to think of themselves as mature, even when they lack some very basic capacities. This can trap a nonprofit in a lower stage of development that, ultimately, has potential to grow even more in furthering its mission. As programs expand during an organization's adolescence, the board and senior staff will want to focus on how to extend the group's reach while maintaining and improving program quality. Program expansion can allow a nonprofit to serve more clients or customers in an existing service area or expand its reach by taking a successful program to a larger scale. Yet, growth is usually a risky endeavor and, if not paced and managed well, can sacrifice program quality and jeopardize an organization's financial health. A careful analysis is necessary to determine whether it is better — or not — to undertake every opportunity that presents itself to augment programs. It is one thing to run a Head Start center serving a clientele of preschoolers; it's something else to expand that effort into a job-training program for youth and adults.

TO GROW OR NOT TO GROW?

Most directors instinctively view any growth as something good. Here are some examples to illustrate nonprofits that chose slow– or no–growth as the right path in advancing their missions more effectively:

- A university research program decided to limit its student body size to 30 in order to maintain the close, congenial, and cooperative work atmosphere for its students on which its reputation was built.

- A drug rehabilitation center chose to accept only a limited number of cases to keep the client-caseworker relationship personal and individualized.

- A day-care center, offered a major contribution to construct a soccer field, refused the donation because it was not appropriate for the population (toddlers) it served.

- A community-development organization declined to merge with a similar group in its city because it might have weakened the strong ties with its local constituents.

- A professional training organization opted to upgrade its infrastructure rather than expand its client base in order to better serve fewer clients, rather than stretch limited resources to inadequately service an increased number.

- A nonprofit theater declined to consolidate with another theater in the city so as to maintain its avant-garde repertoire and brand. Instead, it negotiated reciprocal visiting agreements.

- A health-care center eliminated its cardiac department because a local university hospital provided competitive and high-quality cardiac services.

In adolescence, a nonprofit will typically begin achieving successful short-term outcomes for its clients. As Exhibit 7 on page 24 illustrates, a nonprofit group is ready to move into maturity when program staff and volunteers are delivering quality services, demand for those services is outpacing capacity, and the organization has sufficient resources to continue building capacity and to expand delivery of quality programs.

✓ **Check off the capacity building activities and transitional milestones your nonprofit has accomplished**

Mission-based Focus: refinement of programs and services through experimentation; short-term outcome achievement for clients

Goals: to understand what it takes to deliver the assumed right *quality* of programs and services (i.e., "best practices"); to have the necessary resources to delivery the right quantity of services every time; to have the capacity to manage the use of program resources.

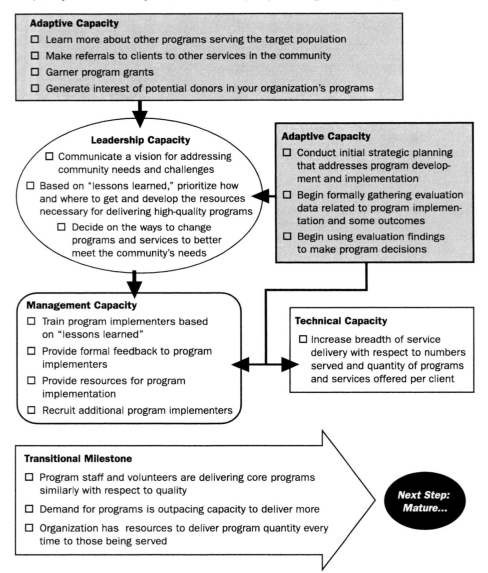

Adaptive Capacity
- ☐ Learn more about other programs serving the target population
- ☐ Make referrals to clients to other services in the community
- ☐ Garner program grants
- ☐ Generate interest of potential donors in your organization's programs

Leadership Capacity
- ☐ Communicate a vision for addressing community needs and challenges
- ☐ Based on "lessons learned," prioritize how and where to get and develop the resources necessary for delivering high-quality programs
- ☐ Decide on the ways to change programs and services to better meet the community's needs

Adaptive Capacity
- ☐ Conduct initial strategic planning that addresses program development and implementation
- ☐ Begin formally gathering evaluation data related to program implementation and some outcomes
- ☐ Begin using evaluation findings to make program decisions

Management Capacity
- ☐ Train program implementers based on "lessons learned"
- ☐ Provide formal feedback to program implementers
- ☐ Provide resources for program implementation
- ☐ Recruit additional program implementers

Technical Capacity
- ☐ Increase breadth of service delivery with respect to numbers served and quantity of programs and services offered per client

Transitional Milestone
- ☐ Program staff and volunteers are delivering core programs similarly with respect to quality
- ☐ Demand for programs is outpacing capacity to deliver more
- ☐ Organization has resources to deliver program quantity every time to those being served

Next Step: Mature...

Program growth presents inevitable challenges for staff, executives, and board members. During adolescence, the staff size usually increases to handle the expanding program workload. As the staff grows, the chief executive will need to consider creating a more hierarchical staff structure with some centralized management. Program staff will need to become more specialized and their job descriptions will therefore be more detailed. The chief executive will most likely begin hiring professional managers who may not directly deliver services but will supervise those who do. At a growing multiservice agency, for example, a trained business manager may be more suitable for an administrative post than a social worker.

Organizational expansion almost always presents staff with big challenges — to assume new responsibilities or a heavier workload, or to operate in unfamiliar settings. Some employees may experience mounting frustration, confusion, and burnout as demand outstrips capacity or services are redirected. Staff managers can head off some of these difficulties by seeking staff input and then communicating decisions openly, particularly with respect to reallocation of existing staff members and hiring of new ones. This was the case at the Trust for Public Land, for example, in the mid-1990s when it shifted its program focus from acquiring land in rural areas to partnering with local parks groups in urban areas, necessitating the development of new skills by staff to serve the new clients.

Expansion of staff, changes in job descriptions, and implementation of more formal systems associated with larger organizations may discomfit and dismay some existing staff. Managers may need to assist staff members in coping with these changes and, for those staff who are not able to adjust and grow with the organization, to provide an exit from the nonprofit. Likewise, board members may need to make a similar evaluation of the chief executive and fellow board members to determine if they are capable and desirous of growing with the organization. Conducting a regular board self-assessment will help the board come to terms with whether or not board members are satisfied with their own service and the work of the board as a team.

The flexibility and casual atmosphere that were positive benefits to an organization during the beginning phase may act to destabilize and undermine it as it moves through adolescence into maturity. As staff size grows, efforts to bolster management capacity become important. With a rudimentary organizational hierarchy, the chief executive and any existing human resource staff should provide for new staff orientation and training, and establish simple personnel policies. It is during this phase that staff and board members can expect a culture change in that teams or divisions are formed and more formal methods of communicating, such as holding regular staff meetings and documenting and disseminating meeting minutes, are necessary.

Growth challenges in the adolescent stage not only affect the staff, but also their leader, the chief executive. Many nonprofits experience a crisis when the role of the chief executive begins to change — as it inevitably will. Board members will need to begin working with senior staff to define the role of the top executive. The chief executive often faces difficult transition problems as the organization grows from adolescence into maturity. He or she will often struggle with the necessary shift from an entrepreneurial to a managerial role, and may be reluctant or unable to lead expansion into new and unfamiliar areas, triggering a leadership crisis. The chief executive may need or want to delegate authority but may have personal difficulty relinquishing control. There may be a need for stronger management, but the chief executive may not be interested in — or capable of — providing it. The founder of a growing performing arts center, for instance, may be a great artistic director but a mediocre theater manager.

VISIONARY VS. MANAGER

Sometimes the attributes of visionary and manager reside in the same individual; more often, different people will be needed to provide both inspiring leadership and solid management.

Typical *visionary* characteristics and qualities include

- the ability to attract followers and motivate people
- the ability to focus on the big issues
- the desire to make effectiveness a top objective
- the capability to set direction
- a willingness to take calculated risks

Typical *manager* characteristics and qualities include

- the ability to create results
- a natural attention to detail
- the ability to focus on processes and efficiency
- the capability to implement strategic guidelines
- a gift for solving problems
- the facility to manage personnel
- the ability to focus on stability

If the staff leader is also a founder, he or she may struggle to distinguish between his or her personal needs and those of the organization (see "Founder's Syndrome" on page 55). In these cases, the board may face the difficult task of determining if the current chief executive is capable of growing and changing with the organization — or if a new chief executive with different capabilities is needed. The board can prepare itself for these tough decisions by assessing the performance of the chief executive on an annual basis and creating a succession plan.

CASE STUDY: GROWING THE MARYLAND FOOD BANK

The Maryland Food Bank typifies many of the growing pains associated with the adolescent nonprofit, such as the departure of a founding staff leader, strategic program expansion, and formalization of systems.

The Maryland Food Bank began in 1979, when Ann Miller, the founder, and a dedicated group of volunteers joined together to provide emergency food assistance to the hungry and homeless. They procured surplus food from food companies, restaurants, and wholesale markets and distributed it to soup kitchens, emergency shelters, senior centers, and day care centers that fed low-income people in the state. The organization expanded gradually over its first several years, as it opened a warehouse, hired paid staff, and extended its services, delivering about 400,000 pounds of food annually.[11]

But when founder Ann Miller stepped down in 1986, the board was faced with the need to select a new staff leader, expand management, and create a strategic plan for growth. They chose Bill Ewing, who had started as a volunteer, to be chief executive of the burgeoning group. Although he was not an experienced manager, he was capable of growing into that role over the next decade: "I went through several wrenching experiences when I had to learn how to manage in a different way," Ewing observed. "When an organization's needs change and a leader doesn't have those skills, … you don't have to automatically leave. That's where professional development comes in," he continued.[12]

When the staff increased to 35 people, Ewing and the board realized that they needed to set up more formal systems for work flow, evaluation, and management. Ewing wrote job descriptions so that staff members had a clear sense of their responsibilities. He also established policies and procedures to coordinate program operations more efficiently. "Organizations that cling to a way of doing things because it was so much fun are the ones that work themselves into trouble," Ewing noted.[13] It was a time of some turmoil as a few employees resisted being held accountable in a more hierarchical system. Nevertheless, most staff stayed and went on to flourish inside the new system.

Creating a strategic plan under Ewing's and the board's guidance also helped the Maryland Food Bank manage its growth. The plan became a blueprint for expanding services, improving quality, and altering the organizational structure. A major part of the plan was an unusual change in the structure of the executive leadership: The board established co-directors, allowing Ewing to focus on external relations and the co-director to concentrate on internal management and operations.[14]

By 1997, the Maryland Food Bank had an operating budget of $1.9 million and was delivering more than 11 million pounds of food to 45,000 people annually. It recently moved its operations to an 86,000-square-foot warehouse, eight times the size of its former facility. Today, it is a high-functioning model of an organization that has transitioned into its mature stage.[15]

Moving through adolescence and into maturity requires continual learning, careful planning, and ongoing program refinement. The chief executive should be capable of making management improvements, planning effectively, and delegating wisely, as Bill Ewing did for the Maryland Food Bank. Meanwhile, the board spends less time on day-to-day operations and focuses more on strategic planning, oversight, and fundraising. The Maryland Food Bank successfully transitioned because its leaders learned to embrace change and allow the organizational culture to shift as part of its growth.

---

11. Stainburn, Samantha. "Growing: When It's Time for Your Start-Up To Grow Up." *Who Cares*. Sept./Oct. 1997.
12. Ibid.
13. Ibid.
14. Ibid.
15. Dembeck, Cher. "Food Bank, with Help from Other Banks, Finds County Home." *The Daily Record*. April 20, 2004.

MATURE

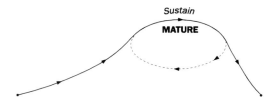

Building on the tendency for young nonprofits to consider themselves mature organizations too early on, it is not until a nonprofit's programs are established and well-regarded in the marketplace or community, its operations and systems are formalized, and its executive and board leadership capable of directing a complex organization, that an organization can validly be said to have entered maturity. For typical nonprofits, that will normally occur sometime after five or six years of operations and when the budget exceeds one or two million dollars.

The savvy nonprofit that reaches this milestone will strive to sustain itself in maturity and avoid lapsing into decline, in the same way that an older person can aim to remain young at heart.

ROLE OF THE BOARD: A GOVERNING BODY

As a nonprofit enters maturity, the board typically further reduces its operational role and increases its policy, oversight, and fundraising functions. The board usually expands and becomes more diverse and more specialized. A regional or national membership association with local chapters will want to assess how its affiliates are to be represented on the governing body.

The board expands and formalizes its committee structure, possibly also creating advisory councils. The strong, independent committees or temporary task forces, along with the officers or a small executive committee, provide any necessary staff consultation between board meetings. On an ongoing basis, new leadership is groomed at the board and committee levels. New members are added to reflect changes in the community or client base, to tap new skills that are needed, and to obtain fresh perspectives.

The board periodically measures whether the chief executive has the ability to sustain, adapt, and manage the organization in its maturity, and, if necessary, hires a new chief executive who is more able to do so. A good executive, likewise, will be aware of his or her own strengths and limitations and seek out and work with board and senior staff members who provide complementary skills and talents.

Board members take time to reflect regularly on the impact of the organization and its programs and ensure that the organization stays focused on fulfilling its purpose, avoiding the mission drift that often occurs in middle age. The mature board continually assesses its own performance and modifies its composition, roles, responsibilities, and structure to stay effective.

Assessing and Fine-Tuning Capacity: Maintaining Relevance and Adapting to Change

Adaptive capacity — the ability of a nonprofit to monitor, assess, respond to, and stimulate internal and external changes — is the key to sustaining an organization in maturity. Even more so than in other stages, adaptive capacity is necessary to successfully negotiate the mature stage — and to maintain the organization in that optimal phase for as long as possible. No enterprise can afford to follow the same course in perpetuity, no matter how sound its original mission. Each year, the ground shifts a little, different needs arise, and new players emerge in the field. For immigrant-support organizations, for example, new waves of refugees arrive every decade and new providers mobilize to help them. To stay relevant, a mature organization continually assesses itself; evaluates its programs; scans the outside environment; and broadens and deepens connections with community leaders, funders, and constituents.

A durable nonprofit organization requires strong leadership capacities in its board members and executive staff. The board and chief executive can learn about changing needs through their broad relationships and deep roots in the external environment, along with formal, in-depth needs assessments. Based on this information, the organization identifies comprehensive needs for improving its management and governance. Additionally, by conducting strategic planning on a regular basis, an established nonprofit can coordinate programs, keep its capacities aligned, and remain on the cutting edge. By communicating and networking with other organizations in its community and field, it can also test methods of mutual collaboration and generate new approaches to better meet the needs of society. The mature nonprofit also has formal systems for periodically evaluating and documenting programs so that successes are internally replicated and transferred to other programs.

The chief executive of a mature organization will need to be adept at managing a large staff and complex finances. He or she builds a strong senior management team, perhaps including a chief operating officer, and will typically be proficient in directing a sophisticated operation. For example: The director of a large, established community-development corporation may require management and banking experience rather than hands-on housing construction or grassroots-organizing experience.

The chief executive must be able to communicate the organization's vision — and inspire staff with it. He or she initiates and leads the process to evaluate and refine programs and to assess the organization on an ongoing basis. He or she also needs to establish clear goals for organizational learning, ensure that developed knowledge is shared internally, and support efforts to identify and apply promising practices in the field. The chief executive will usually play a prominent leadership role in mission-related advocacy efforts in the community.

The mature nonprofit builds its management capacity by hiring program specialists, trained managers, and other specialized, professional staff. It has formal training activities, evaluation processes, and personnel policies. In addition, the organization has advanced methods for communicating among staff, such as utilizing a management reporting system, staff meetings at the departmental and organizational levels, and a staff newsletter or monthly update. The organization also maintains a well-developed financial-management system that, if necessary, is capable of managing a capital budget, cash reserve, or endowment.

As the staff size of a mature nonprofit increases, the organizational structure becomes increasingly hierarchical, with a larger number of professional managers and specialized program staff. A small, private college entering maturity, for example, will require whole departments that have nothing to do with academic research or teaching, but instead handle areas such as human resources, facility management, and public relations. The organization's more centralized and hierarchical organizational structure has a clear division of labor and reporting relationships. Mature membership organizations with local affiliates will establish a centralized organizational structure and determine how much autonomy affiliates will have.

Staff members of an established organization require regular training, retraining, and skill upgrades in order to be able to do their jobs well. Communication between staff members needs regularity and clarity — through team meetings, project timeline distribution, and circulation of important documentation. Together, they need to remain focused on achieving overall organizational goals — not just the objectives of their department, unit, or program area.

A mature nonprofit is also careful to strengthen its technical capacities. It is able to regularly and systematically evaluate programs and document its program models. Based on what it learns from the evaluation as well as assessments of changing needs, the organization alters and improves its technical support functions. It upgrades marketing skills to communicate its activities through a well-developed Web site, newsletter, and annual report. If it hasn't already, the mature nonprofit will want to undergo a branding campaign so that it may achieve general public recognition as a notable, worthwhile, and professional organization.

Most important, the established nonprofit takes care to develop its fundraising capacities so that diverse and stable streams of revenues are available to sustain it in maturity. It not only cultivates existing income sources, but also works to attract new sources of funding. It may plan to secure its financial future by building a cash reserve or endowment, or by conducting a capital campaign for institution-building. It might even pursue new earned-income ventures. Financial managers will also develop contingency plans for different economic scenarios.

SUSTAINING THE ORGANIZATION IN MATURITY

It is clearly possible to sustain an organization in the mature stage in perpetuity — although doing so is no easy job. It requires a constant reinvigoration by the board and chief executive of mission, leadership, adaptability, resources, and program quality.

The goal is not simply to maintain a nonprofit's equilibrium at the "peak" of the curve. The dynamic, mature nonprofit must also strive to extend its life curve on a permanent upward plateau as it encounters new opportunities and overcomes new challenges. The ability to adapt becomes the most important capacity for a mature organization — it is impossible for an organization to avoid stagnation if it cannot adapt to change. To avoid stagnation, a mature organization continually monitors and evaluates its work, and stays in tune with the needs and perceptions of the outside environment. The organization's leaders should constantly be aware of internal and external shifts in order to keep the organization adept and its mission needed.

EXHIBIT 8: MATURE PHASE: BUILDING CAPACITIES TO EFFECTIVELY DELIVER PROGRAMS

✓ **Check off the capacity-building activities and transitional milestones your nonprofit has accomplished**

Mission-Based Focus: program achievement of expected longer-term client outcomes; "going to scale" with respect to program implementation (directly through own programs and indirectly through partnering with other organizations) such that community impact increases over time

Goals: to understand what it takes programmatically (quantity and quality) to achieve outcomes; to have the necessary resources to deliver the right quantity and quality of services every time; to have the capacity to manage the use of program resources and quality of program delivery; to leverage other organizations' resources for program delivery

Adaptive Capacity
- ☐ Forge strategic alliances with other nonprofits to provide services and programs
- ☐ Develop sustainable resources for long-term program and service delivery through diversity of revenue sources
- ☐ Engage in community-level decision-making bodies that make and/or influence policies affecting program and service resource allocation

Leadership Capacity
- ☐ Based on "lessons learned," prioritize how and where to get and develop the resources necessary for delivering high-quality programs
- ☐ Decide on the ways to change programs/services to better meet the community's needs

Adaptive Capacity
- ☐ Strategic planning decisions about programs/services incorporates formal program learning
- ☐ Evaluation systems in place to assess and monitor inputs, program quantity, program quality, and client outcomes
- ☐ All programmatic decision-making includes discussion of evaluation findings

Management Capacity
- ☐ Improve training and development of program implementers based on "lessons learned"
- ☐ Develop formal tools and process for providing feedback to program implementers
- ☐ Conduct regular assessments of program staff resource needs
- ☐ Develop formal strategies for recruiting strong program implementers in the future

Technical Capacity
- ☐ Increased breadth and depth of service delivery with respect to numbers served, quantity of program and services offered per client, and quality of programs and services

Transitional Milestones for Continued Maturation
- ☐ Program staff and volunteers are consistently improving the quantity and quality of service delivery based on formal learning processes
- ☐ Organization has resources to deliver better program quantity and quality every time to those being served
- ☐ Organization is achieving community impact through programs as well as partnerships and alliances

Next Stage: Maintain Mature State

or...

Next Stage: Stagnant

During the mature stage, a nonprofit organization needs to understand what it takes to consistently deliver the right quality and quantity of services and to achieve longer-term client outcomes. As described in Exhibit 8, adaptive capacity will enable an organization to sustain itself in maturity by consistently improving the quantity and quality of programs, developing the resources to support them, and achieving greater community impact.

CASE STUDY: SUSTAINING THE FOUNDATION CENTER

The Foundation Center epitomizes the mature, seasoned nonprofit institution that has sustained itself in that stage. It has established credible programs and developed efficient operating systems. It has also diversified its revenue streams, conducted an ongoing strategic planning process, and has adapted quickly to external changes in its environment.

The Foundation Center was incorporated in 1956 in New York City by a small group of foundation leaders in the wake of a series of congressional hearings on foundations that were critical of the secrecy — financial, programmatic, and governance — that was common to most foundations of the time. To alleviate congressional and public criticism, the Center's mission was to collect, organize, and publicize reports and information about U.S. foundations, both their finances and their programs. In its first decade, the Center built an impressive library collection of books and printed materials and augmented it with current data on foundation finances and activities.

In 1960 it published its first Foundation Directory, with detailed information about 5,200 foundations, and began the bimonthly Foundation News, with a listing of current foundation grants. During the 1960s, the Center developed partnerships with public and academic libraries to make its publications more widely available. The Center grew dramatically in the 1970s and 1980s, expanding its base of support and supplementing it with earned income, using computer technologies to manage and disseminate foundation information, and establishing field offices and cooperating collections around the country.

The Foundation Center faced and surmounted the challenges of each decade by keeping its adaptive capacity strong through a regular strategic planning process (about every three years).This allowed the board and senior staff to periodically step back and take a broader view of where the Center has been, is now, and wants to be in the future. In its most recent plan, for example, the board and staff have outlined strategies to widen its work to cover more dimensions of philanthropy, to extract more value from its information resources, to help grantseekers and grantmakers work together more effectively, and to improve public discourse about critical issues in philanthropy.[16] (And the board is now preparing for its next strategic forecast, which will culminate in a revised plan in 2006, the Center's 50th anniversary.)

Over the years, the Foundation Center's leaders have likewise been careful to stay abreast of technological developments to keep its programs vital and useful. It has enhanced the way it collects and communicates information, conducts research, and provides education on the grantseeking process, harnessing new technologies and responding to market demand. In 1994,

---

16. The Foundation Center. "Moving the Field Forward: Toward Greater Accountability and Effectiveness in Philanthropy." (Strategic Plan for 2004-2006.)

for example, it recognized the potential of the Internet to further its mission and quickly developed a strong online presence. Since online demand skyrocketed, the Center has maintained a strong competitive edge by rapidly converting its operations and information to convenient electronic formats. The Center also developed the management capability necessary to administer 150 staff, offices in five cities, cooperating collections in 230 locations, and more than 30,000 daily visitors to its Web site.

Most importantly, the Foundation Center maintained necessary funding to sustain its programs by developing a sound and reliable mix of both earned and contributed revenues. The Center's annual operating budget is now approximately $16 million, with grants from foundations and corporations making up about 40 percent of its revenues, and sales of its print and electronic resources and fee-based educational programs providing the other 60 percent. Its strong revenue stream has enabled it to maintain many free programs and research collections as well.

With the media, government officials, and the public calling on foundations to operate more effectively and transparently, the Foundation Center has positioned itself to remain relevant and healthy within the context of its main mission to strengthen the nonprofit sector by advancing knowledge about U.S. philanthropy.

The Foundation Center matters more than ever because it remains one of the nation's leading authorities on information about grantmakers. The Center has stayed vibrantly mature for almost 50 years by continually assessing its performance and the changing needs of its market. Based on this knowledge, it has responsively modified its programs and business model, while achieving financial sustainability.

Stagnant

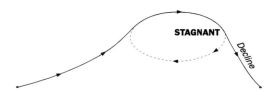

Each year, hundreds of nonprofits start or tumble down the slippery slope to stagnation. Savvy board members or executives can recognize the signs: Funding support diminishes, demand for services wanes, the number of volunteers declines, staff morale suffers, and key leaders and managers leave the organization. Sometimes a nonprofit descends rapidly into this crisis. At other times, the decline can take years as the organization begins to wither almost imperceptibly. And, it is very important to understand that stagnancy can occur at any stage, from start-up through maturity.

Identifying Stagnancy

The clearest indication of an organization flirting with stagnation is its lack of adaptive capacity. This usually is a direct result of problems with the board or executive leadership. Board members may become unenthusiastic and minimally involved. Or the same few board members may show up at every meeting to dominate decision making and to rehash settled issues. Board decision making may be stalled by excessive procedures or complex committee processes. The board may be further hampered by an outdated structure, a neglected nominating function, low board turnover, and a lack of new, invigorating members. Typically, board members' program oversight declines and communication with staff diminishes.

Concomitant with the degeneration of adaptive capacity, weakened leadership capacity usually occurs and accelerates a nonprofit's slide into stagnancy. A chief executive that stays past the point when he or she can provide fresh insight, approaches, and vision is an all-too-common scenario. This situation can prove disastrous when the leader cannot foresee or is incapable of providing a plan to address a sudden, compelling crisis, such as new competition or a major loss of funding. The problems arising from executive shortcomings can be worsened by a board that does not recognize these problems or act to correct them.

Stagnant nonprofits typically evidence much complacency. Board members and chief executives are often in denial that their organization is declining and becoming less effective. They avoid risks and lack innovative decision making. Almost always, a declining organization has let its core capacities and culture weaken. Individual programs become fiefdoms focused on departmental goals, rather than organizational ones. In particular, organizational assessment, program evaluation, strategic planning, and knowledge management are usually inadequate.

The deterioration often surfaces when a nonprofit organization loses touch with its market. When there are changes in demand, the economic environment, or competition, it has no mechanism to detect these changes and so cannot modify existing programs or create new ones. Instead, the organization continues to deliver a fixed menu of the same old — and perhaps obsolescent — programs. The first sign for an ossified trade association, for instance, may be a decline in the number of members that are renewing, indicating it is no longer serving the needs of its constituents. Public television stations offer another good example of this malady: During the late 1980s, most were blindsided by the rapidly expanding cable industry, which provided similar programming. Public television stations were slow to respond to for-profit cable offerings like the Discovery Channel, A&E, or Bravo, and so lost significant numbers of viewers to their competitive offerings.

Frequently, the well-developed management systems of a mature nonprofit deteriorate into "red tape" that bogs down the organization. Some old and large international relief groups, for instance, have been slow to modernize systems and adapt new technologies. Their desire for maintaining the status quo has prevented them from being flexible and responsive.

In a stagnant organization, employees often fragment into cliques and turf battles among managers become common. This is a confusing and stressful time for employees. As their morale wanes, staff turnover may increase. Top performers may burn out and consider leaving. Meanwhile, poor performers become entrenched and all staff members find themselves in a day-to-day scramble to react to emergencies, rather than do their work proactively — and do it well.

A declining client base, poor performance, and unclear goals inevitably translate into financial difficulties. Long-term supporters may cut back or pull out and few or no new revenue sources are cultivated. The organization often tailors existing programs solely for the purpose of matching funders' special interests, or the organization responds to requests for proposals indiscriminately, whether or not they fit its mission. Consider the case of the large but aging social-service agency that continually chases dollars by inventing new initiatives primarily to attract available funding. Oftentimes, financial systems and controls are weak and the organization does not comprehend the deterioration in its financial position until disaster is upon it. Ultimately, cash reserves may become insufficient and the organization starts falling behind on its financial obligations.

Again, these are signs of stagnation that can occur at any stage of organizational development — and to which directors and chief executives should be alert at all times. The case study on the next page illustrates one organization's battle to stay afloat.

CASE STUDY: THE DANCE THEATER OF HARLEM: IS THERE HOPE?

The Dance Theater of Harlem demonstrates classic causes of decline in a nonprofit: drastic shifts in the funding environment, an entrenched founder who resists relinquishing control, and a board incapable of exercising authority. As in most stagnant groups, the decline also entailed weak management systems, financial troubles, and diminished staff morale.

Arthur Mitchell rose to fame in the 1950s when he became the first African-American dancer to perform in the New York City Ballet. In 1969, he founded the Dance Theater of Harlem (DTH) to provide a home for dancers of color to perform classical dance. DTH soon became a world-renowned, artistically dynamic ballet company that grew and thrived in its first decades.

Although undoubtedly the guiding spirit and visionary of DTH, Mitchell and his board were unable to sustain the capacities needed for a mature organization. The New York Times *noted that Mitchell "is an artistic genius, but has no real knowledge of management, and isn't willing to relinquish any control over his organization."[17] That weakness — and the DTH board's inability to address it — led to a series of crises, beginning in the 1990s when a cash shortfall and funding loss from the National Endowment for the Arts forced DTH to close down for six months. The emergency sale of two of DTH's buildings and bail-out grants from foundations and individuals ended the cash crisis.[18]*

Yet this financial reprieve was only temporary because the underlying causes were not addressed. Although Mitchell did hire a professional manager in 2001, the person left after only a few years.[19] Meanwhile, the board of directors declined disastrously from 17 to 4 people, with the board chair resigning in 2003.[20]

External events plagued DTH as well. After the September 11, 2001, terrorist attacks in New York, earned and contributed revenues for performing arts declined drastically. Without a board or management team to meet these challenges, DTH was forced to reduce its $10 million operating budget by $3 million and to lay off 19 of its 27 staff members, keeping only the dancers on the payroll."[21] By 2004, DTH was forced to slash another $2 million in operating costs and spend its $2 million endowment to pay off loans and operating costs. Not long after, DTH terminated its remaining employees and was left only with volunteers to continue its once-vaunted programs.

The Dance Theater of Harlem's prospects seem bleak — but there is hope for revival. Despite its problems, DTH continues to perform internationally, to receive universally enthusiastic reviews, and to generate earned revenue.[22] Throughout its time of troubles, Arthur Mitchell nevertheless maintained the quality and vibrancy of DTH's programs. And Mitchell, who is 70 years old, now seems more willing to make the changes necessary to rescue DTH: "It's time for me to move over ... to bring in a partner who is savvy, who can put together a working board, who has the clout internationally to bring money and infrastructure."[23] DTH recently received $1million from its new chair, philanthropist Catherine Reynolds. Her desire to support DTH confirms that some people still see a need for DTH in the community.

It is not impossible to reverse stagnation once the slippery slope has been touched. If a proactive (rather than reactive) leader can move quickly to identify the problems and make the necessary changes, along with board and staff, the organization may be stabilized; it may find its appropriate place again in society; and obsolescence can be avoided.

---

17. Pogrebin, Robin. "Deficit Threatens Dance Troupe in Harlem." *The New York Times*. May 26, 2004.

18. Souccar, Miriam Kreinin. "Dance Theater May Bow Out in Fiscal Crisis." *Crain's New York Business*. April 19, 2004.

19. Ibid.

20. Ibid.

21. Haughney, Christine. "New York Arts Groups in Dance for Survival." *Washington Post*. April 28, 2003.

22. Kaufman, Sarah. "A Ballet Stretches to the Limit; Famed Harlem Troupe Pursues Financial Security, New Director." *Washington Post*. June 2, 2004.

23. Pogrebin, Robin. "Deficit Threatens Dance Troupe in Harlem." *The New York Times*. May 26, 2004.

REVERSING STAGNATION

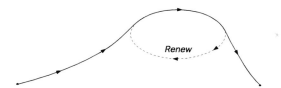

Renew

The Dance Theater of Harlem represents the classic dilemma for boards and executives of nonprofits in the stagnant stage: Can the stagnation be reversed and the organization returned to health and vitality? Or must it inevitably decline into obsolescence and become defunct?

The good news is that it is often possible for even seriously ailing organizations to renew themselves. The bad news? It is a difficult, sometimes unpleasant, and usually thankless job to accomplish. It requires a board of directors who can candidly assess the organization's problems, refocus the group on its mission and clients, and create and market a realistic plan to stabilize and revive the organization. In some cases, the turnaround effort involves significant budget cuts, rebuilding programs, and altering missions. Sometimes the organization may even find it necessary to revert to the start-up or adolescent stages. In other cases, the nonprofit is able to return intact to a healthier state of maturity. Sometimes, the reversal of stagnancy can be accomplished by merging with another group. A preventive health-care group and a community-health clinic that are both languishing, for example, might choose to join forces to offer a revitalized continuum of care that is more financially and managerially viable.

ROLE OF THE BOARD: INITIATING A TURNAROUND

The board, with cooperation and support from the chief executive, is usually required to take the first steps to initiate the resuscitation process. Because adaptability and leadership are so often at fault, the board often must begin by shaking itself up. Board leaders may want to retire some disengaged veteran board members and add new board members who will support the renewal effort. Board development will need to be directed toward bridging skill gaps, removing unproductive members, and creating new structures and processes to improve decision making and performance. New board members who function well in adverse circumstances and who savor a challenge should be sought out.

Officers will want to discuss with each board member the level of commitment that will be required of him or her during the revitalization phase. Out of that process, some board members may resign voluntarily and new members with critical expertise and energy can be recruited to replace them. An ideal new member will have creative ideas for reviving the organization and can provide access to resources necessary for that revival. The board's structure and processes may also need to be redesigned to reflect present-day needs.

A competent and committed board can generate new energy and leadership by working with staff to identify alternative program strategies through strategic and business planning processes. To improve a stagnant organization's prospects, it will most likely be necessary to develop new programs or revise or eliminate some existing efforts. This process might reasonably begin with a reassessment of market need. Programs can then be evaluated in light of their utility in serving important constituencies and their performance. What are the outcomes, and are these sufficient? Which elements contribute to the program's success — or failure? The findings can lay the foundations of a plan for reshaping programs to better meet needs and fulfill the organization's mission. Unlike the mature stage of an organization, this is the time for the board to be active and involved — sometimes very hands-on — in order for the organization to achieve the necessary turnaround.

REBUILDING CAPACITY

The most important core capacity that a stagnant organization must transform is its adaptive capacity. A reviving nonprofit revamps this capacity by re-examining constituents' needs and re-establishing connections with clients, community leaders, and funders. It must also acknowledge the need for organizational renewal, candidly appraise itself, and create a turnaround plan. The organization stabilizes financially by restoring the confidence of dedicated funders and enlisting the support of new ones.

For failing organizations, it is almost always essential to review and rebuild leadership capacity. Though the board can initiate and motivate changes to reverse a nonprofit's decline, the crucial component is good leadership at the chief executive and senior-staff levels to implement change. A flexible and motivated chief executive could possibly stay at the helm and effectively help renew the organization. But if the current staff leader bears significant responsibility for what ails the nonprofit — and this is often the case — the board needs to seriously consider relieving the top executive and hiring a new chief executive who can act as a change agent to lead the revival effort. A full-scale turnaround for an organization in an acute crisis may be best led by an energetic new chief executive with a different perspective, novel ideas, and skills in crisis management. Yet, regardless of who manages the turnaround effort, the board needs to provide its full support and confidence if this difficult work is to succeed.

If senior managers and the board have difficulty thinking creatively about revising the mission or approach, a nonprofit organization may want to enlist the assistance of an external consultant to generate innovative alternatives and provide objective perspectives. An outside advisor can be especially helpful when some board members or senior staff members are in denial about the seriousness of problems. The professional outsider's sober and objective candor can provide the impetus for changing attitudes, even if staff and board don't particularly like what they are told.

Programmatic shifts usually require new skills and operational support — which may mean changes in staffing and management structure. Management capacity is shored up by organizational leaders revising staff job descriptions and restructuring departments to reflect the renewal plan. The chief executive will be primarily responsible for implementing these changes. Retraining or reconfiguring existing personnel is often a viable option. At other times, starting with a clean slate may make most sense, despite the challenge of transitioning staff in a time of crisis. Leaders also need to comprehensively review the organization's infrastructure in light of changing programs and technologies. If administrative systems are needlessly complex, confusing, and outmoded, new procedures need to be created.

In a declining organization, financial instability is usually one of the first visible signs of difficulties. Therefore, one of the crucial jobs for the board and top management is to stabilize and then expand the nonprofit's financial base. Usually, financial management systems and controls also need to be revamped. At the beginning of the recuperative process, when cash-flow problems and budget deficits may exist, the organization will need to pare expenses. After the nonprofit's mission is clarified and programs revised and made more relevant, board and top staff then need to concentrate on finding funding opportunities that clearly fit the new direction. One effective fundraising strategy is to utilize the nonprofit's new plans for improvements as the focus of fundraising; another is to re-engage long-term supporters who have made significant investments in the group in the past. For example, one funder, who had a deep commitment to a youth-service organization that was in distress, proved to be an effective ally by offering advice drawn from his experience with other grantees, by making referrals to management-assistance providers, and by giving the struggling nonprofit grants for consulting services. In some cases, an especially supportive and sophisticated funder can champion an organization's plan for rejuvenation and encourage other funders to provide support.

At the same time, however, previous funding sources should not be overlooked and best efforts made to convince them to continue funding the new mission. Board members can play an important role in stabilizing the finances of a nonprofit by reassuring prior funders of the renewed soundness and stability of the revitalized organization — as well as by reaching out to new funders.

The revitalized nonprofit also retools its technical capacity. One of the most important capacities that may need revitalization is communications. During a stagnant period, an organization's reputation may be diminished and there may be confusion about its mission and programs among outsiders, including funders, collaborating organizations, and constituents. Messages about noteworthy activities, changes, and accomplishments need to be conveyed effectively to key audiences in order to restore confidence. The non-profit should market its revised programs and services and communicate honestly and clearly with outsiders about its ongoing renewal. Here, again, the board can play a major supporting role in reassuring important outsiders of the viability and continued usefulness of the organization.

Other technical capacities that are important during this period are legal skills, which may be necessary in order to renegotiate debt with creditors, legally restructure the group, or terminate contracts or leased space.

Ultimately, to rebuild its capacity to effectively deliver programs, a nonprofit organization needs to re-examine its programs' relevance to the community and revise those programs to improve their quality. As Exhibit 9 illustrates on the next page, the milestones for renewal are the awareness that programs are declining; returning to effective delivery of services; and obtaining sufficient resources to do so.

EXHIBIT 9: REVERSING STAGNATION BY REBUILDING CAPACITIES TO EFFECTIVELY DELIVER PROGRAMS

✓ **Check off the capacity-building activities and transitional milestones your nonprofit has accomplished**

Mission-Based Focus: re-examination of how to make programs relevant to the community; through program innovations and changes, return to a level of high-quality, outcome-focused programs and services

Goals: to reassess community needs for current programs and services; make program refinements to meet current community needs

Adaptive Capacity
- ☐ Conduct formal community needs assessment
- ☐ Reach out to community leaders to assess target population needs
- ☐ Reconnect with funders to inform them of current challenges with programs and services and communicate plans for change
- ☐ Reduce role as community resource for other nonprofits' program delivery and/or
- ☐ Reduce role at community decision-making and/or policy-making bodies until programs have improved

Leadership Capacity
- ☐ Have program leadership role take precedence over community leadership
- ☐ Challenge current assumptions about programs and services
- ☐ Make effective, evaluation-based program decisions on the ways to improve programs and services to better meet the community's needs

Adaptive Capacity
- ☐ Conduct external evaluation of program quality and outcomes to identify recommendations for improvement
- ☐ Modify evaluation systems to ensure that they are measuring what matters

Management Capacity
- ☐ Hire new program implementers and fire poor performing program implementers
- ☐ Improve program implementer professional development efforts
- ☐ Improve feedback tools and processes for program implementers

Technical Capacity
- ☐ Increase breadth and depth of service delivery with respect to numbers served, quantity of programs and services offered per client, and quality of programs and services

Transitional Milestone for Renewal to Adolescence
- ☐ Awareness that programs are declining
- ☐ Program staff and volunteers are delivering sufficient quantity and quality of programs and services
- ☐ Organization has adequate resources to effectively ? deliver services

Next Stage: (Re)Growth or...

Dissolve and Become Defunct

MOVING FORWARD

Once a plan for renewal is outlined, it is important to develop a realistic schedule for its implementation. The decline of an organization usually takes place over a period of time; there is no reason to expect that reversing that process could or should happen overnight. Since most organizations cannot be turned around on a dime, patience is an important virtue for all those involved.

During the renewal process, it is important for executives and the board to foster a culture in which employees can feel comfortable voicing their concerns. The chief executive helps by connecting staff to the new mission and vision of the organization. Staff successes and contributions should be celebrated and widely disseminated among employees. Team work and internal communication are most important in this pick-up phase, and all members of the organization should be aware of and in favor of the plan for renewal.

CASE STUDY: RENEWING THE NEW-YORK HISTORICAL SOCIETY

The New-York Historical Society is a model of a nonprofit that managed to reverse its decline by reinvigorating executive and board leadership, consolidating and overhauling programs, and revamping fundraising efforts.

For 188 years, the New-York Historical Society was one of the most revered repositories of the nation's history. The Society's vast collection of books, manuscripts, maps, photographs, and documents was a key resource for pre-Civil War national history, as well as for New York City and State historical archives. The Society encompassed a library, museum collection, and an historical archive.

But in 1993, the venerable — but notoriously cash poor and inadequately governed — institution closed its doors to the public. Its physical plant was dilapidated, library items were poorly catalogued, works of art and artifacts were neglected, and funding to maintain operations was exhausted. All public programs were ended, more than half the staff was dismissed, and it seemed like the end was approaching for this esteemed institution.

The Society's salvation came in the form of capable new leadership and a major refocusing of programs — some of them controversial. The Society's board acted swiftly to bring in a talented new chief executive to lead an organizationwide effort to evaluate its problems, refocus its mission, revise programs to meet market needs, and restore the confidence of funders.

For example, the Society raised $16 million by deaccessioning duplicate materials and pieces unrelated to its mission and used those funds to build an endowment to support ongoing operations. Betsy Gotbaum, the Society's vigorous new chief executive, cut the annual operating budget while acquiring capital development funds. With $12.6 million from the city and state, she initiated reno-vation of the Society's landmark building on Central Park West, including the main exhibition galleries. In addition, the Andrew W. Mellon Foundation funded a collaborative effort between the Society's library and that of New York University to eliminate the inadequate cataloging of the Society's acquisitions. The Mellon grant also permitted the library to restore its public hours to 30 per week. By the end of the 1990s, the New-York Historical Society had restored itself to a healthy and sound mature organization.[24]

In 2005, the New-York Historical Society celebrated its bicentennial as an archive of national importance — an event that some in 1993 would have thought unlikely. But when the decline of the institution was forcefully brought to the attention of the Society's board, they reacted — belatedly but swiftly — to save the institution by rejuvenating both leadership and mission.

---

24. David Dunlap. "Historical Society Shuts Its Doors but Still Hopes." *The New York Times*. February 20, 1993; and Paul Goldberger. "To the Rescue of a Grande Dame of Museums." *The New York Times*. June 12, 1997.

Defunct

DEFUNCT

Although the verdict is still out on whether the Dance Theater of Harlem can replicate the success of the New-York Historical Society in reversing its decline into stagnancy and obsolescence, there are nevertheless literally thousands of other nonprofits across the nation that close their doors every year.[25]

In a few situations, a group may disband because it has actually fulfilled its mission, such as an organization whose goal to eradicate a disease is accomplished when a cure is discovered. In most cases, however, nonprofits dissolve for less-positive reasons, such as loss of a compelling mission focus, a chronic inability to operate programs effectively, or a lack of technical expertise in marketing and fundraising.

There is no moral judgment inherent in the demise of a nonprofit. As in the for-profit world, the existence of constant change in the makeup of the nonprofit sector is natural and healthy, just as there is constant change in the world around it. Indeed, some observers have even argued that struggling groups that languish for a long time before expiring should instead act more expeditiously on their own to close down so that the resources they consume can be utilized by organizations that are more successful in achieving their missions. The attrition rate for new for-profit corporations exceeds 10 percent a year, five times higher than nonprofits, indicating that there may be some validity to this viewpoint.

In actuality, the problem may not be that some nonprofits become obsolescent and die, but that there is no established and legitimized path for those nonprofits to follow when their time to depart has come. It is past time to recognize that nonprofits can and should be able to exit gracefully and honorably.

Role of the Board: Taking Care of Business before Saying Good-Bye

How do the organizational leaders determine when is it best to pull the plug, rather than attempt resuscitation? There are no hard-and-fast rules, but these considerations are paramount in the decision:

- The nonprofit's programs are widely considered to be ineffective and its client base has declined significantly.

- The board of directors is moribund, taking little interest in the problems of the organization and evidencing no will or ability to initiate needed change.

---

25. According to William Bowen in *The Charitable Nonprofits*, the exit rate for 501(c)(3) organizations during the 1984-1992 period averaged 2.3 percent per year and was even higher for younger nonprofit organizations.

- The current chief executive is likewise incapable or unwilling to take on the task of resuscitation and the board can find no one to take on this job.

- Funding is declining and long-time supporters are drawing away; no new funding to support rehabilitation and change efforts is readily available.

- The organization's public reputation is poor and seems beyond resurrection.

- Management systems are not supporting the organization's work.

Sometimes it comes down to a decision by the board as to whether, all things considered, the organization has any remaining potential to do at least as good a job as other competing organizations that are striving to meet similar needs. If the answer is "no," then the organization's mission is unlikely to be achieved and its resources and staff would be better utilized by another, healthier organization.

Although the decline into obsolescence usually occurs over a period of time, sometimes one significant change, internal or external, is all that is needed to send a distressed operation into a swift downward spiral. For example, an organization slowly losing touch with its clients' needs and seeing its programs concomitantly lose their effectiveness, could be thrown into irreparable downturn by loss of its founding chief executive or by a competitor receiving a major grant to expand its programs. Valuable staff and board members start to leave, a culture of crisis paralyzes remaining staff, long-time funders pull back, and the organization implodes.

USING CAPACITY FOR A SMOOTH ENDING

Upon reaching the decision to terminate the life of an organization, however, there are capacities unique to the final stage of the lifecycle that must be recognized by the board of directors and utilized in the last stage of the lifecycle. The organization still needs the adaptive capacity to wind down operations responsibly. Appropriate staff leaders will want to assess the needs of its remaining clients, refer them to other programs, and transfer any residual, functioning programs to other organizations if possible. Ideally, the board would document in writing what has been learned through the full lifecycle of the organization and share this information with key constituents and competitors.

Although terminating an organization inevitably causes morale and motivation problems, senior staff and board members will try to manage the dissolution process strategically and conscientiously. The organization has obligations to staff, to creditors, to funders, and to the public that must be recognized. For example, the dissolving organization should terminate staff respectfully and with a strategic eye to keeping the organization functioning until the chosen end date. Board members and the chief executive should candidly inform funders and similar groups about plans to end their programs.

Organizational leaders will want to consider strategies for shifting any remaining resources to other nonprofits and meet with community leaders to determine how best to meet or transfer, if possible, the ongoing needs of the clients that were being served. For example, in 2004, the San Francisco-based Management Center, which provided management assistance to other nonprofits, decided to cease operations. It employed a competitive process to award its best and intact programs to the Georgia Center for Non-profits, CompassPoint, and the Center for Nonprofit Management in Southern California.

Meanwhile, the board and chief executive must assess the extent of the organization's legal and financial obligations and make careful plans to meet them, such as settling outstanding contractual obligations, making sure that final bills are paid, and distributing any remaining assets. If the organization has significantly more liabilities than assets, professional legal counsel will be necessary in order to arrange an orderly and court-supervised dissolution of the corporation and its assets.

Leadership capacity is deliberately and methodically dismantled during this period. If the chief executive completes his or her duties related to the dissolution, he or she may leave the organization. The board is usually the last remaining vestige of the nonprofit, surviving until all tasks necessary for dissolution have been accomplished, and then formally and legally ending the corporate life of the nonprofit.

CLOSING THE DOORS

A voluntary exit requires that a nonprofit

- Adopt and record a board resolution to dissolve the nonprofit corporation.

- File articles of dissolution with the office of the secretary of state.

- File a public notice of the dissolution of the organization.

- Liquidate all liabilities and pending claims according to law.

- Distribute all remaining assets according to the articles of incorporation or state law.

- Notify all important stakeholders.

- Dissolve the board.

ACKNOWLEDGING THE END

If it is appropriate, organizational leaders may want to hold some ceremony or event to acknowledge the organization's accomplishments and successes during its life span. This could be especially meaningful for the founders, long-time staff, clients, and stakeholders.

Case Study: Dissolving the YWCA of Waukesha County

The example of the YWCA of Waukesha County illustrates the responsible way to terminate a defunct organization.

The YWCA of Waukesha County in Wisconsin, which was founded in 1920, originally served nonworking wives and working younger women. By its fifth decade, it was the ninth largest YWCA in the nation with more than 8,800 members.[26] But the descent into stagnation began in 1988 with the departure of long-time executive director, Beverly Chappie. Instability in the top job (five directors averaging only three years each) followed, contributing to declining programs, loss of contact with members, and a deteriorating physical plant. Earned and contributed revenues steadily declined and the YWCA struggled to balance its budget as membership plummeted. As one former member explained, "I got fed up with a dirty locker room, and, frankly, found better facilities at the YMCA."

The final straw came in early 2004, when the Waukesha YWCA lost its funding from the Waukesha Housing Authority and its latest executive director resigned. The board then made a last-ditch, desperate effort to resuscitate the organization by expanding the mission to serve boys and men and launching a $250,000 fundraising drive.[27]

But the board was unable to meet the fundraising goal and attract the executive talent necessary to revitalize the YWCA. By July 2004, the board recognized that it needed to cease operations. During the next few months, it transferred programs and referred members to other agencies. It then entered into receivership, a state court proceeding similar to bankruptcy,[28] and transferred control of its $73,000 endowment fund to another nonprofit to use for similar charitable purposes. A thoughtful $65,000 gift enabled the YWCA to pay employees for their final weeks of work in dissolving the organization.[29] The YWCA's board will liquidate its remaining financial obligations through the sale of the YWCA building, estimated to be worth about $2 million.[30]

The YWCA was a stagnant organization whose board determined that leadership, management, and technical capacities were inadequate to the task of salvaging the organization. The board acted responsibly and promptly in terminating the nonprofit — thereby freeing up community resources for other nonprofits that were better able to meet community needs.

---

26. Walker, Laurel. "Hoping for a Miracle, Expecting the Worse." *Milwaukee Journal Sentinel*. June 10, 2004.

27. Epstein, Reid. "County Adopts 'All-Inclusive' Mission." *Milwaukee Journal Sentinel*. February 13, 2004.

28. Walker, Laurel. "YWCA Is Left Hopeless with Hopeless Outlook." *Milwaukee Journal Sentinel*. June 17, 2004.

29. Doege, David. "YWCA Board To Find Agency To Take Over Fund." *Milwaukee Journal Sentinel*. August 11, 2004.

30. Kogutkiewicz, James. "YWCA Pays Its Workers." *GM Today*. September 11, 2004.

At this point, the reader should have a good sense of which stage of the lifecycle best describes his or her organization and whether the core capacities in each stage are well-aligned. Now is a good time to ponder the questions below — perhaps also using the lifecycle assessment tool in Appendix 2 — to assess a nonprofit organization more thoroughly and accurately.

QUESTIONS FOR THE BOARD AND CHIEF EXECUTIVE

- Overall, which lifecycle stage best describes your organization?

- Is your organization moving from one stage to another? If so, does it have the requisite capacities to make that transition successfully?

- Which stage does your organization want or need to evolve into?

- How can the board and chief executive collaborate better to assess the organization and plan for improvements?

QUESTIONS FOR THE BOARD

- How does your board need to change so that your organization can effectively advance or sustain itself? Specifically, what type of executive development do board members need?

- How can your chief executive improve so that your organization can progress or sustain itself? Or does your organization need a new staff leader to take it to the next stage?

QUESTIONS FOR THE CHIEF EXECUTIVE

- Is your relationship with your board one that is conducive to building adaptive and leadership capacities?

- How does your own performance need to be enhanced so that your organization can effectively evolve or sustain itself?

- How does your staff need to change so that your organization can progress or sustain itself?

- How do your organization's management systems and operations need to improve? What else is important to change (e.g., program evaluation, knowledge management, financial management, etc.) in order for your organization to effectively advance or sustain itself?

3.
Building Organizational Capacity

After reading the last chapter, most board members and chief executives could probably place their nonprofit organization somewhere along the continuum of lifecycle stages and assess their organization's capacities. Usually, the areas that need improvement are inter-related. As naturalist John Muir observed, "as soon as you start to tug on one part of nature, you realize it's connected to everything else." Similarly, once an organization begins to focus on capacity building, it will initiate activities that strengthen its capacities in weak areas, and these improvements will reinforce other capacities even further — thereby helping the nonprofit to better fulfill its mission no matter what stage of the lifecycle it is in. And, by enhancing organizational capacities, the transition from one lifecycle stage to another can be more smoothly accomplished.

In Chapter 2, the most common capacities for each stage were described in general terms. This chapter will discuss the core capacities in more detail, and explore how board members and executives can build and strengthen them as their organizations grow and change.

ESSENTIAL COMPONENTS OF ADAPTIVE CAPACITY

It is critical for board and staff leaders to pay attention to adaptive capacity throughout an organization's entire lifespan. Why? Because adaptive capacities are paramount — if they are weak, it will be difficult to advance in the management and technical areas and move forward to new lifecycle stages. Organizations demonstrating good adaptive capacity have cultures where staff and volunteers at all levels are encouraged — or even required — to be critical consumers of information, to experiment with new ideas and approaches, and to contribute to the organization's continual self-evaluation. Highly adaptive nonprofits are always scanning and monitoring the outside world to follow trends and to keep abreast of opportunities. They are inquisitive about their programs and operating environments, and use that knowledge to inform their plans. They also employ tools effectively to make decisions and secure and maintain resources to serve the mission.

The essential components of adaptive capacity are

- needs assessment

- organizational assessment

- program evaluation

- knowledge management

- strategic planning

- collaborations and partnerships

While it is the chief executive or senior staff who often conduct the actual examination and oversee each of these areas, it is incumbent on the board of directors to ensure that work on each of the components is regularly undertaken in a thorough and professional manner — and to participate in them where appropriate.

Needs Assessment

Regularly assessing the needs of people who benefit from a nonprofit's work can keep its programs dynamic and relevant. Staff members can conduct formal needs assessments to better understand variations in demand. Market research methods such as surveys and focus groups facilitate gathering quantitative and qualitative data from a wide range of people and sources, which, depending on the organization's mission, could include neighborhood residents, current and potential audience members, scholars in a particular field, companies in an industry sector, or children of a certain age and socioeconomic background.

Staff can also learn about needs through informal means. Professional networks, colleagues, funders, and local policy-makers can be used to discover trends in the operating environment. Also, local universities, colleges, and other research centers may have community data that could be valuable in assessing demand. Board members, the chief executive, and sometimes senior staff should exchange information on a regular basis about shifting needs in the community or appropriate field of work.

Needs assessment data can guide program planning efforts. For a growing arts group in the adolescent stage, the information could be used to design cultural programs that are responsive to new and wider client bases. If the group is a mature or stagnant after-school program, needs assessment can help identify programs that could be eliminated or modified, thereby keeping its programs relevant. A survey of members can provide a trade association with valuable data to inform the design of membership benefits.

Organizational Assessment

A formal organizational assessment holds a mirror up to a nonprofit and allows the leadership to evaluate the group — board and staff. Sometimes an assessment only examines one aspect of an organization, such as governance, but it often involves a comprehensive review of the entire organization. In any case, it can help diagnose capacity-building needs and create a plan to build on strengths and address weaknesses. Frequently, an organizational assessment, coupled with an external environmental review, is the initial step in a strategic planning process. If organizational reviews are conducted regularly, a baseline against which to measure developmental progress over time can be established.

There are many organizational assessment instruments available in publications or online that can be self-administered by board, executives, staff, or an outside consultant. (Some of the more popular ones are distributed by Maryland Association of Nonprofits, the Leader-to-Leader Institute, and Venture Philanthropy Partners. The TCC Group also provides an organizational assessment tool based on the four core capacity models described in this book.) Full participation and discussion about the findings and meanings will make the assessment worthwhile. Alternatively, or in conjunction with an organizational self-assessment tool, outside consultants can be utilized to gain the benefit of an outsider's expert, objective opinion. The consultant will typically conduct a set of confidential interviews and discussion groups with stakeholders and then give a report of discoveries to key board and staff.

The nature of the organizational assessment depends on a nonprofit's developmental lifecycle stage. When performed for a start-up, it may be as simple as a few reflective discussions among volunteers and board members that clarify organizational needs and priorities. But if a nonprofit is faltering, it may be a more complex, in-depth exercise that alerts the board and executives to how and why an organization has stagnated and what may be done to restore its vitality. Even a mature nonprofit will need to conduct organizational assessments — a requirement that many leaders of mature organizations often overlook.

PROGRAM EVALUATION

Periodic evaluation of each specific program will ideally be conducted throughout an organization's entire lifecycle, but especially at junctures when key organizational and programmatic decisions are being made. Systematic, outcome-based evaluations can inform the program staff members about *what* strategies are working, *how well* they are working, and *why* they are performing well. Program evaluation is more than just an accountability tool for funders. If done properly, it encourages a wide group of the organization's stakeholders to better understand program quality and the progress toward achieving outcomes.

Using a logic model that outlines in detail the specific methods that an organization is using to achieve its desired outcomes can be helpful. This model shows relationships between short- and long-term outcomes, the program strategies or activities and their outputs, and program inputs or resources.

Program evaluation does not need to be an elaborate, time-consuming process, but it does need to be conducted regularly. Emerging organizations, especially, need to keep evaluations simple since they tend to have many competing demands and only limited resources. Larger, more-established nonprofits may choose to devote extra resources to hiring staff evaluation specialists or outside evaluators.

KNOWLEDGE MANAGEMENT

Conducting needs assessments, organizational assessments, and program evaluations does not give a nonprofit's leaders all the information they need to be successfully adaptive. Knowledge management — distilling and integrating knowledge accumulated by the board and staff members and putting that knowledge to work to improve the organization's adaptive capacity — is another key component of adaptive capacity.

What is the best way to manage a nonprofit's knowledge? First, there should be a plan for collecting information — data and the conclusions drawn from them by staff and board — in a user-friendly manner. Next, organizational leaders, stakeholders, and constituents can analyze the information, run data analyses, draw conclusions, and most importantly, suggest changes. Finally, the findings, insights, and recommendations should be utilized by board and senior staff: incorporated into decision-making processes for board meetings, strategic planning efforts, program development sessions, staff meetings, and collaborations with other groups.

The following types of information should be gathered and managed appropriately: changes in the nature of the problem that an organization is attempting to address; the resources available; research and promising practices in the field; and information about the quality, quantity, and outcomes achieved by the nonprofit's programs.

DATA ➤ INFORMATION ➤ KNOWLEDGE ➤ ACTION

The following example elucidates the differences among data, information, knowledge, and action.

Data provide raw numbers, pure facts. *Example*: Demographic survey results arranged in a spreadsheet indicate that there are 1,000 homeless individuals in the county.

Information categorizes data, extrapolates patterns. *Example*: When analyzing the numbers in the spreadsheet, it becomes evident that among the homeless there are a significant number of young Latino women with children under the age of five.

Knowledge combines different sources of information and distinguishes a relationship or a cause and an effect between them. *Example*: Even though the county has a Planned Parenthood program, a women's shelter, a soup kitchen, and a community-health clinic, none of the services is specifically catering to the needs of the growing Latino population. Materials are available only in English and staff members in these facilities are white males who primarily speak English. Therefore, the county has a growing societal dilemma that has gone unnoticed and has reached serious proportions.

Action makes use of knowledge by making it productive. *Example*: A nonprofit allocates funds to hire bilingual female employees at each county facility serving the homeless, publishes written materials in Spanish, and creates a task force to encourage the various services to collaborate with each other in order to fully reach the Latino community.

STRATEGIC PLANNING

Assessments, evaluations, and knowledge-gathering are most useful when brought into a strategic planning process to help an organization identify its unique strengths and weaknesses, clarify the key issues it faces, and develop strategies that make the most efficient use of its human, financial, and program resources. It can also provide a nonprofit's leaders with a better understanding of the external environment in which it operates — especially identifying unexplored opportunities and challenges. Most important, strategic planning provides an opportunity to examine the nonprofit's mission and to determine whether that mission is still a relevant and achievable one.

How elaborate should a strategic planning process be and what outcome might be expected? It depends on where an organization is in the lifecycle. It can be as simple for a start-up group as gathering the leaders on a Saturday afternoon to set some goals for the next year and make a to-do list on a flip chart to achieve those goals. For an adolescent organization, a strategic plan would typically be a more detailed blueprint for expansion, with long-term goals and an implementation plan for reaching those goals. Strategic planning for a mature or for a reviving, stagnant organization tends to be more complicated and time-consuming, involving many more stakeholders and can lead to intricate, multiyear plans for sustaining or reviving the organization. The information gleaned from needs assessments, program evaluations, organizational assessments, and knowledge management processes should all be put to use in the strategic planning effort.

WHO PARTICIPATES IN STRATEGIC PLANNING?

Strategic planning is always a team effort and it is important to ensure that all stakeholders in the organization have the opportunity to play a role, regardless of the size and age of the nonprofit:

- The **board** sets the direction for the organization and therefore must ensure that the plan will be viable and able to serve as the guide and benchmark for future decisions. **Individual board members'** perspectives add to the relevance of the plan.

- The **chief executive** is usually the driver of the planning process. He or she ensures that the board is ready and prepared. He or she is the chief communicator and manager of planning. The chief executive also ensures that the final goals will be met according to expectations.

- **Staff members** provide informational support, keep the goals grounded, and implement the plan through day-to-day operations.

- **Clients** and **customers** are invited to express what they need or expect from the organization and to provide feedback on quality of service.

- **Funders** have a stake in the success of the organization and therefore may be asked to articulate indicators that, from their perspective, will define the nonprofit's progress in implementing its plan.

- An **outside consultant** may serve as a facilitator who ensures that the process is followed, who is fair in guiding the process, and who incorporates all the participants' points of views.

COLLABORATIONS AND PARTNERSHIPS

The resources of other nonprofit organizations, government agencies, and private companies should not be overlooked when building adaptive capacity. By networking, collaborating, and creating strategic alliances with other groups, a nonprofit can tap into these outside resources, including staff time, expertise, space, and equipment available from others.

The best way to identify potential collaborators is for the board and senior executives to maintain strong, ongoing relationships with colleagues in the community. By being an important and audible voice in the community on issues central to an organization's mission, potential partners are more likely to be approachable about and agreeable to collaborating.

Start-up organizations may do quite well by informally cooperating with other nonprofits to share information and make cross-referrals. An adolescent group may forge more formal collaborations that entail well-defined, mutually beneficial relationships to achieve common goals. Established or declining nonprofits may consider even more strategic restructuring options, like mergers, joint ventures, and administrative consolidations.

SHOULD A MERGER BE CONSIDERED?

If some of the following conditions exist, it may be time to consider a merger:

- The merger recommendation is the result of a careful and conscientious study defining the future needs and mission of the organization.

- There are too many organizations in the area with the same mission, delivering quality services. Competition has become counterproductive.

- It is difficult to run the organization efficiently or effectively. Key resources, skills, or tools are not readily available.

- Merging with another organization would broaden the mission and enable the new organization to offer a full or wider range of services to constituents.

- Another organization is offering to merge and this would allow the board's vision for the future of the organization to more rapidly become a reality.

- No other solution except dissolution seems viable.

LEADERSHIP CAPACITY: GUIDING THE ORGANIZATION TO ITS FULLEST

Adaptive capacity is predicated on excellent board and staff leadership. Well-led nonprofits tend to have high-performing boards, leadership succession plans, and strong partnerships between the chief executive and board members.

In general, outstanding leaders create a vision, set goals and priorities, devise plans for achieving those goals, and inspire others to get the necessary work done. They consistently assess their own progress in order to make better, more strategic decisions moving forward. They know that strong programs are only made stronger when staff members have the information they need to make wise decisions. Outstanding leaders are also willing to learn, share information, and use data to make midcourse corrections toward the common purpose. They gain the respect of other leaders in their community and field, persuading and leading them — along with those inside the organization — to take action.

These necessary leadership qualities can be improved through board development, executive leadership development, and well-managed leadership transitions.

BOARD DEVELOPMENT

The first step to strong board leadership is for the members to conduct a candid board self-assessment annually. Do board members know and adhere to their basic responsibilities? Do they each attend meetings regularly? Does the board as a group select the chief executive and assess his or her performance, ensure that the organization has adequate resources to achieve its goals, adhere to legal and ethical standards, and maintain accountability? Are board members given an orientation that reviews the roles and responsibilities of members and that includes the organization's history and financial position? Are board members given opportunities to be trained in good governance principles and effective group decision-making processes? And are members given regular briefings on specific programs — especially their connection to mission and results — so that they can make informed decisions about them?

Based on the answers to the above questions, the board can create a thoughtful plan for improvement. The plan may involve adjusting the composition of the board, clarifying and changing roles and responsibilities, or altering board structure. If a board needs new members or members with certain expertise, identifying the gaps and then strategically filling those slots will alleviate that problem. Associate work groups or advisory councils can serve as training grounds and feeders to the board. At the end of each member's term, a candid evaluation should be made of the contribution of that member; underperforming members should not be automatically re-elected. The needs of an organization's board change through each stage of the lifecycle; therefore, membership turnover is not an unhealthy characteristic.

FINDING THE RIGHT BOARD MEMBERS

Recruiting the right board members requires asking probing questions of potential candidates. For example:

- Why do you want to join our board and what do you expect to gain out of this partnership?

- Why do you want to serve on the board rather than help the organization in some other way?

- What is your understanding of the mission of the organization and how will you be able to further it?

- What can you offer this board? What unique skills, experience, or talents do you bring?

- What is your understanding of your duties and responsibilities as a board member and are you comfortable with those expectations?

- Do you have any previous board or other volunteer experience, especially with nonprofits?

- Can you commit the time, energy, and money required to serve on this board?

Likewise, the board's role changes as the nonprofit's lifecycle evolves: During a nonprofit's start-up stage, board members usually need to play a hands-on role and sometimes are responsible for day-to-day operations and program delivery. As a nonprofit's staff expands during adolescence, board members shift to overseeing staff or managers and gradually divest themselves of direct management responsibilities. The board of a mature nonprofit concentrates on advisory, planning, fundraising, and general oversight functions. Board members may need to return to more hands-on participation and direct roles when attempting to turn around a stagnant nonprofit or when shutting one down.

EXECUTIVE LEADERSHIP DEVELOPMENT

The type of executive leadership needed at each stage of the organizational lifecycle also varies. If a nonprofit is in infancy or adolescence, it might benefit most from entrepreneurial or charismatic visionary leadership: a board leader or chief executive who can attract resources and build the organization. A mature organization usually requires a chief executive more adept at guiding professional managers, establishing systems, formalizing operations, evaluating and refining programs, and maintaining the vision and mission of the organization. A group in stagnation may need to return to entrepreneurial or visionary leadership that can make the tough decisions necessary to resuscitate the organization, while inspiring new confidence within and without the group.

Nevertheless, there are some common characteristics of outstanding executive leaders at all stages of a nonprofit's lifecycle. He or she at all times works closely as a team with the board to plan for the future; set agendas; act as ambassadors for the organization; and generate revenues from individual donations, private or corporate foundation grants, and government contracts. The executive collaborates with the board to articulate an organizational vision and then motivates staff to achieve it. A good chief executive surrounds himself or herself with staff possessing complementary talents, who share an ability and commitment to anticipate and plan for change, and who use sound information to help make decisions.

An outstanding chief executive will strive to create a synergistic relationship with the board chair. A good executive-board chair relationship is like a good marriage: It is based on mutual respect, trust, commitment, and effective communication. The two need to keep each other informed of major developments in their two realms: the governing board and the working staff. The chief executive needs to be involved in any board development process, and the board chair must be kept abreast of major developments in the chief executive's areas of responsibility.

How can a chief executive develop leadership abilities? The first step is for the executive to assess — either alone or with the help of the board — his or her leadership strengths and limitations. Customized training, coaching, or mentoring are then available to strengthen leadership. Some chief executives benefit most by working with or consulting their peers in other nonprofits. For a staff leader who is overworked or burned out, a sabbatical or other opportunity to reconnect with his or her career passion can reinvigorate leadership in a nonprofit.

The development of a synergistic board-chief executive partnership should be an ultimate goal for any nonprofit organization. Board members and executive leadership need to work together to plan, set agendas and policies, raise money, and live as ambassadors for the organization.

LEADERSHIP TRANSITIONS

Leadership transitions are critical times for both the board and staff. But while they can be stressful and disruptive, if properly managed, they also present unique opportunities to review mission and direction and to set new courses of action.

Throughout the entire lifecycle, board leaders will want to consciously cultivate the next generation of board leadership. Most board members have the potential for assuming a leadership position in some area during their tenures. Career paths can be created to offer potential board leaders a chance to participate in different areas and to take on more responsibility over time. Committees of the board can be used as a way to foster responsibility and experience in emerging leaders. Term limits for officer positions should be adhered to in order to permit other potential leaders to grow and flourish on the board.

In the same vein, the board needs to plan for succession in executive leadership. Most chief executives would agree that, if they were suddenly incapacitated or removed entirely from the scene, their organizations should be able to continue operations with the least amount of interruption possible. While such a contingency can rarely be completely planned for, particularly if the chief executive is the founder or has been with the organization for many years (see "Founder's Syndrome" below), the wise nonprofit board will make a genuine effort to anticipate its options if this occurs — intentionally or unintentionally.[31] Ideally, there will be a clear and understood process for finding the next leader and anticipated processes for dealing with the transition, both internally and externally.

FOUNDER'S SYNDROME

Founder-led nonprofit organizations face distinctive challenges as they evolve. Terms like *founder's syndrome* or *founderitis* have been coined to explain the symptoms exhibited when a founder's personality and dominance begin to adversely affect the organization. In her article, "Founders and Other Gods," Deborah Linnell describes the common "can't live with 'em, can't live without 'em" nature of the situation. She notes that many of the strengths of founders — their dynamic purposefulness, courageous ability to take risks, and drive to succeed for the sake of the mission — contribute greatly to success during the start-up period when flexibility and informality reign.[32] But these very assets can become deficits later as the nonprofit expands and formalizes. A crisis can result if board or staff members sense the need for more rigorous systems, management, and planning, but the founder resists delegating, relinquishing some control, and changing. Too often, this leads to the founder being forced out or, in the worst case, to the disintegration of the organization altogether.

Linnell observes, however, that not all founder transitions need to be so disruptive. In some cases, the founder is able to develop leadership skills that grow in tandem with the needs of the organization and can subsume his or her personal needs and interests in favor of the organization's needs and interests. When this seems possible, the board will want to actively support the founder's efforts to improve his or her shortcomings and to obtain professional or consultant guidance. The board can encourage the founder to hire top staff who will complement his or her strengths and board members can show by example how to share ownership of the organization. The founder of a college that served working adults, for example, evolved with the help of the board into a role as the keeper and inspiration of the organization's vision and values, while being supplemented by a dean with a broader set of necessary management skills.

However the situation unfolds, it is the board's ultimate responsibility to ensure a succession that will enable the nonprofit to move on and flourish when a founder leaves.

31. Redington, E. and D. Vickers. *Following the Leader: A Guide for Foundation Director Transition.* Columbus, OH: The Academy for Leadership and Governance, 2001.

32. Linnell, Deborah. "Founders and Other Gods." *Nonprofit Quarterly.* Spring, 2004.

© 2006

Once it becomes clear that there is or will soon be a vacancy in the top executive leadership, the board needs to act quickly and decisively to devise a recruiting and interviewing plan. This will likely include a special board committee, which produces a revised job description focusing on what the organization currently needs in a chief executive — although the drafters will want to be careful not to make the document simply a reaction to the strengths and weaknesses of the outgoing staff leader. The committee can interview prospective candidates and make recommendations to the full board.

In the adolescent and mature stages of an organization, the most common reason for a transition is that the chief executive is burned out or is no longer the right fit for the organization's needs at that stage in development. New executive leadership is often needed in order to turn the organization around if it has become stagnant and a decline seems unavoidable. Some boards face the founder's syndrome: when the personality and desires of the founder are overly identified with and too predominant within the organization. In this sensitive case, personal relationships and loyalty to the chief executive are often emphasized at the expense of budgeting, strategic planning, accountability — or even the very mission of the organization.[33]

Exhibit 10 below provides a causation matrix for executive leadership transitions in a nonprofit and suggests possible outcomes.

EXHIBIT 10: ASSESSING THE CONTEXT OF EXECUTIVE TRANSITIONS

		Chief Executive's Situation		
		Chief executive likes job and wants to stay	Chief executive likes job but wants to leave for a better opportunity	Chief executive does not like job (is burnt out, has outgrown job, etc.)
Organization's Situation	**Chief executive is the right fit for organization**	Chief executive stays	Board convinces chief executive to stay; or board needs to find new chief executive	Make improvements to chief executive's situation (e.g., sabbatical); or chief executive leaves and board finds replacement
	Chief executive may not be the right fit, but may be able to change to become a better fit	Chief executive needs to change to meet organization's needs; or board terminates chief executive or asks for resignation and hires replacement	Chief executive performance needs to improve if he/she will stay; or chief executive leaves and board hires replacement	Chief executive leaves; board finds replacement
	Chief executive is not the right fit	Terminate chief executive or encourage chief executive to leave, or ask for resignation; board finds better replacement	Let chief executive leave or encourage him or her to do so; board finds better replacement	Let chief executive leave or encourage him or her to do so; board finds better replacement

33. McNamara, Carter. *Founder's Syndrome: How Corporations Suffer-and Can Recover.* 1998. www.mapnp.org/library/misc/founders.htm; and Stevens, Susan Kenny. *Nonprofit Lifecycles: Stage-Based Wisdom for Nonprofit Capacity.* Cleveland, OH: Stagewise Enterprises, 2001.

MANAGEMENT CAPACITY: DIRECTING AND SECURING ORGANIZATIONAL RESOURCES

Management capacity is directly linked to leadership capacity since executive leaders often serve as direct managers of staff. Board members and the chief executive will want to provide sound direction to managers so that they can allocate organizational resources efficiently. Managers need to be guided by clear organizational priorities in order to make effective decisions about hiring, training, organizing, assessing, and rewarding staff and volunteers. Capably managed nonprofits engage staff and volunteers in problem solving, and provide the necessary support for them to carry out their work and have clear communication channels. The board will often play only an oversight role in this capacity, ensuring that the chief executive and senior staff take the necessary steps to grow the management capacity as appropriate for each stage of the lifecycle.

Management capacity can be fortified through human-resource development and management, internal communications, and financial management.

HUMAN-RESOURCE DEVELOPMENT AND MANAGEMENT

Human-resource management ought to be appropriate for the lifecycle stage and size of an organization. During start-up and adolescence, when there is a smaller number of staff and/or volunteers, normally there is little organizational hierarchy and human-resource management functions are informal. As an organization expands programs and adds new employees, hiring, orientation, training, and performance-assessment processes will need to become more systematized. At every lifecycle stage, however, a regularly updated and widely disseminated organization chart that clearly shows reporting relationships and responsibilities is essential.

The main function of human resources at any stage of the lifecycle is to recruit, nurture, and coordinate competent staff and volunteers who will help an organization achieve its program goals and mission. Salaries and benefits must be sufficiently competitive to attract and retain qualified staff. Staff and volunteers need to understand their roles and responsibilities within the organization and know what performance expectations and goals they will be measured against at periodic performance evaluations. They should receive positive feedback from senior staff and board members on a regular basis, making them feel valued and their work appreciated. Staff members need to be hired, oriented, and given the resources and tools necessary to do their jobs well. They should also be given the opportunity for professional training and development on a regular basis in order to improve their skills and contribute more to their programs. Teamwork and collegial problem solving should always be encouraged.

INTERNAL COMMUNICATIONS

A start-up nonprofit can usually communicate sufficiently by informal conversations among board, staff, and volunteers in the hall or around the lunch table. But internal communication methods — to ensure adequate information flows down the organizational chart from managers and upwards from the staff — usually need to become more formal as an organization moves through adolescence and into maturity. Without such mechanisms, staff and volunteers may work at cross-purposes with the leadership because of inaccurate assumptions and inadequate guidance.

There are many ways to maintain and improve communication within a nonprofit. One of the most basic is to establish and distribute a manual that sets the policies and procedures of an organization in writing. The management structure should also be clear to staff so that communications channels for each staff member or volunteer are evident. As an organization moves through adolescence and into maturity, managers will want to provide more one-on-one supervision and guidance, hold regular staff meetings and retreats, document and disseminate what was discussed at these meetings, and share information via e-mail and staff newsletters. Opportunities are typically provided to staff to reflect on lessons learned from their work and to share this knowledge with other staff members and entire departments. Most importantly, managers should always remember that communication is a two-way process: Managers must be able to listen to staff and accept constructive feedback.

FINANCIAL MANAGEMENT

Every nonprofit, no matter what its size or lifecycle stage, must adhere to an annual budget, keep accurate financial records, and pay bills on time. Ideally for every organization — but a requirement for those beyond the start-up phase — regular financial statements are produced. Leaders then analyze this financial data, such as understanding the unit costs of various programs, and use it to inform their decision making.

The financial management function becomes more structured as an organization evolves. A start-up group may need only to establish a checking account; a one-page, one-year budget; and a simple cash-based accounting system. As an organization matures, multi-year budgeting, an independent audit, cash-flow management, and financial controls are put in place so that the board and senior staff have the financial information they need to make decisions and to fulfill their responsibilities. Financial management becomes even more complex with large, established organizations that may need to manage investments and endowments.

The skills of the person charged with performing the financial management function will typically also evolve with the organization. Start-up and adolescent nonprofits may be able to get along with only a part-time bookkeeper. As a nonprofit grows, its finances may reach the level of complexity requiring a full-time financial manager. A mature non-profit institution most likely will need a chief financial officer and/or comptroller with concomitant and advanced skills.

TECHNICAL CAPACITY: OPERATIONAL FUNCTIONS OF A NONPROFIT

Technical capacity is measured by the skills of a nonprofit's staff members and their ability to carry out particular organizational and programmatic roles. Additionally, the actual tools staff members have available to them are important in measuring and building technical capacity: The staff needs adequate and appropriate technology, equipment, facilities, and program materials in order to bring their skills and talents to bear on achieving the mission. While the board is less involved in these operational functions, it needs to appreciate the importance of technical capacity, to encourage the chief executive's attentiveness in this area, and to be supportive in obtaining the resources to sustain and improve this capacity.

Technical capacity is the easiest of the four core capacities to improve because an organization can acquire — with money or sweat — the staff skills or tools it needs, or obtain training to make improvements in the appropriate areas. Indeed, many nonprofits are led to invest in technical capacity building because it often results in tangible successes that are easily measured.

Technical skills and tools alone, however, are not enough for an organization to be effective. Without leadership to direct these resources, the ability to adapt to changes in technical capacity, and the proficiency to manage these resources, technical capacity is only tangential to the success of a nonprofit. A nonprofit's technical capacity is enhanced by increasing skills in the following:

- service delivery
- evaluation
- outreach and advocacy
- marketing and communications
- earned-income generation
- fundraising
- accounting
- legal matters
- facilities management
- technology

In order to build this capacity successfully, staff with these capabilities are hired, consultants are retained to train existing staff, or more experienced staff members are utilized to train less knowledgeable staff and/or volunteers.

SERVICE DELIVERY

All nonprofit organizations need the knowledge, experience, and skills to implement programs and services in a manner that enables them to maximize impact. A school requires competent teachers to teach the children in its classrooms. Licensed doctors and nurses are needed to effectively deliver the health-care services of a community health clinic. In certain fields, accreditation requirements mandate specific competencies from staff. In any setting, service providers should maintain up-to-date professional knowledge in order to sustain and enhance program quality.

EVALUATION

Skills to evaluate programs and services are another technical requirement. In most cases, these skills will be basic, such as the ability to set measurable objectives, keep track of progress in achieving those objectives, and draw lessons from past experience. As programs become more complex, more sophisticated research design, performance indicators, and analysis skills may also be required of staff members. This tracking and evaluation should be discussed periodically between each staff member and his or her direct supervisor. Progress and growth will help to set goals and objectives for future projects.

Outreach and Advocacy

Some nonprofits, such as community-organizing and advocacy groups, may require strong outreach skills to develop and maintain connections with constituents. All nonprofits can benefit from staff members who have the capacity to become respected and active leaders in their communities or fields.

Marketing and Communications

Marketing skills are crucial for an organization to define, shape, and promote its products and services. These proficiencies include the ability to identify people who need the products or services, to set competitive and affordable prices for them, and to distribute services and products effectively. Communication strategies enable an organization to refine its promotional messages and to convey them effectively to clients, funders, and other constituents.

As an organization evolves, marketing and communication skills may have to be upgraded. While a start-up may be able to communicate sufficiently (via volunteers and/or board members) by word-of-mouth and marketing with a simple brochure, an established organization will require more advanced public relations capabilities and more sophisticated communication vehicles such as an advanced Web site and an elaborate annual report. Adolescent and mature nonprofits will have marketing and communications teams among the staff, with the board mostly providing oversight and signing off on new initiatives and message deliveries.

Earned-Income Generation

Closely linked to marketing, earned income — selling products and services, such as tickets for a play, admission to a recreation center, greetings cards made by a disabled person, or subscriptions to a health newsletter — is an increasing proportion of nonprofit revenues. Generating those revenues requires solid skills in business planning and marketing, either on-staff or on a consulting or contract basis. To run a successful earned-income program, a nonprofit will have to conduct market research to understand the potential demand for new or existing products and services. A solid business plan for such a venture includes realistic financial projections and well-crafted strategies for pricing, promotion, and distribution. More established organizations that initiate earned-income programs will require staff or consultants with abilities in areas such as market research, direct mail, advertising, or e-commerce.

Fundraising

The most common technical capacity that most nonprofits cannot survive without is fundraising. Distinct from earned income, fundraising attempts to raise altruistically motivated donations from individuals or corporations without the corresponding sale of a product or service. Another variant of fundraising is procuring grants from foundations or government agencies, although these grants usually require the delivery of products or services to third parties (often referred to as *deliverables*).

Nonprofits usually find it necessary to build strong skills in researching, identifying, and cultivating prospective funders and donors and in making effective and compelling requests to them for their donations. Likewise, a staff member or consultant experienced in grantwriting and shepherding grant proposals through government and foundation

COMPONENTS OF A BUSINESS PLAN

A business plan is a comprehensive document created for a specific project — for instance, a potential new service — that presents a justification for the proposed project and evaluates the impacts (financial, mission, personnel, etc.) on the organization. The components of a business plan are

- *Executive summary* — a plan overview that answers the questions "who, what, where, why, and how?"

- *Project description* — background information and justification of the new endeavor

- *Market analysis* — summary of the external environment, demands and influences, pricing, and target audiences

- *Financials* — multiyear analysis of revenues, expenses, and projected cash flows

- *Operations plan* — outline of daily activities, staffing, and general procedures

- *Risk analysis* — an explanation of what could go wrong and how to lessen the chance of risks

- *Appendices* — supporting information and documents

bureaucracies is often essential. Board members and executive leaders can — and should — offer much assistance in cultivating and maintaining good relationships with major funders and donors.

Fundraising abilities need to evolve as the organization does. Initially, a start-up group may only secure one major source of funding, but as an organization grows and progresses through new stages, funding sources need to become more diverse and numerous to match the breadth and depth of the organization. The nonprofit that enters maturity reliant on only one funder or source is seriously deficient in fundraising management capacity, no matter how advanced its other capacities may be. Board members and chief executives need to ensure that there is a development plan in place that is scaled to the growth of the organization and that provides for revenues from a reasonable variety of sources. In addition, large nonprofit institutions may also need to be proficient in conducting capital or endowment campaigns.

ACCOUNTING

Every nonprofit requires the skills necessary to adhere to sound accounting practices, whether they are provided by staff or by a contractor. Throughout a nonprofit's life, the board and chief executive are responsible to funders and regulatory agencies for accurately accounting for income, expenditures, liabilities, and assets, and for establishing internal controls to prevent malfeasance and misappropriation, as well as to protect the nonprofit's assets. As an organization matures, it will need to develop more formal and sophisticated accounting systems to track a more complicated mix of revenues and expenditures, restricted grants, reserves, investments, and endowments. Building capacity for proper accounting is one area that is often overlooked by boards and chief executives of growing organizations.

LEGAL MATTERS

Compliance with local, state, and federal laws is a necessity for every organization, from the small local dance troupe to the multimillion-dollar health charity. A start-up usually needs, at a minimum, to create bylaws and articles of incorporation and to obtain tax-exempt status. During expansion, legal issues related to employment, leases, liability, and insurance will arise. Mature nonprofits may need to handle more complex matters, such as joint ventures and trademark and licensing issues. When a nonprofit declines and dissolves, legal assistance is often required to renegotiate debts and terminate contracts and leases. And at every point in the lifecycle, the board and chief executive must ensure that local, state, and federal reporting requirements for nonprofits are met. Until a nonprofit reaches a fairly mature stage, most will utilize outside counsel to handle legal matters.

FACILITIES MANAGEMENT

Throughout its entire lifespan, a nonprofit will need to manage, operate, and maintain appropriate and affordable facilities to house the staff and work of the organization. For a start-up group, this may only entail borrowing or subleasing space in which volunteers can work. For an adolescent or mature nonprofit with the need to house a large staff or work area (such as a clinic, homeless shelter, or a theater), it may mean leasing, purchasing, or constructing a facility. A defunct or declining nonprofit will likely need to consolidate space, sell property, and terminate leases. At every lifecycle stage, a nonprofit's leaders will need to make effective decisions about space usage and affordability.

TECHNOLOGY

A nonprofit must have the capacity to evaluate, operate, and maintain technological systems. Modern technology can immeasurably increase the efficiency and effectiveness of an organization — from telephone systems, to photocopiers, to computers. To be most effective, however, technology must also be appropriate for the needs of the organization. Too often nonprofits waste precious resources on technology, especially electronic equipment and software, that is unnecessary, overly sophisticated, or too complicated for staff to manage.

High-quality technological systems can enable a nonprofit to track, store, analyze, and distribute data related to client needs, organizational functioning, programs, finances, and operating environment. For most nonprofits, staff members, at a minimum, need access to word processing, basic spreadsheets, and e-mail and Internet software — and the hardware on which to run them. As a nonprofit enters adolescence, basic databases, especially for accounting, fundraising, and program management, are typically set up and staff members are trained to use them appropriately. When a nonprofit reaches maturity, it will likely need to install and manage a local area network, as well as advanced software for streamlining communication and analyzing data. Maintenance of most technology systems is handled by contractors or consultants, until the nonprofit grows to a substantial size in adolescence or maturity and the volume of such work expands to the point at which it becomes more cost-effective to hire in-house staff.

This chapter covered the four core organizational capacities in depth, and ways to develop them further. By answering the questions below, readers might identify the top priorities for attention in their specific organizations.

QUESTIONS FOR THE BOARD AND CHIEF EXECUTIVE

- Which specific capacity-building activities are of highest priority for your organization to focus on over the next few years?

- How will you pursue these capacity-building activities, and who needs to be involved in them? In particular, how do board and staff need to work together?

- Do you need outside assistance to build any of the capacities? If so, from whom?

QUESTION FOR THE BOARD

- Does your organization need to prepare for a leadership transition on the board? If so, how will you do this?

QUESTION FOR THE CHIEF EXECUTIVE

- How does your organization need to improve its management and technical capacities? Which particular capacity-building activities do you need to pursue to address these areas?

4.
Taking Capacity Building One Step Further: Obtaining Outside Support[34]

After reading Chapters 2 and 3, readers may have decided that their nonprofit could benefit from improvements in one capacity or another. This chapter briefly explains both the types of services available to nonprofits for making improvements and how to make the best case to potential grantors for funding the effort.

When a board or chief executive has determined that an organization needs to improve an area of capacity, the first question to be answered is: Can this be accomplished by existing board members and staff, or must outsiders be tapped into to provide the needed services? Sometimes, if the board and senior staff have the time, training, and experience, they can accomplish capacity building without outside help or additional expenses. Indeed, some organizational development work is sensitive and confidential and may be better done by those within the organization's culture and structure.

More often, however, a nonprofit needs to turn to outside groups or individuals (trainers, educators, facilitators) to make real progress in capacity building. This inevitably means new expenditures. A nonprofit looking for outside help must initially determine if it can incorporate the new expenses into its operating budget or commit the necessary resources from its unrestricted assets or income. If an organization doesn't choose or cannot afford to fund some or all of its capacity-building needs out of its general revenues or assets, it also has the option to seek funding from grantors to cover the costs. Today, grantmakers are increasingly receptive to proposals for strengthening the infrastructure of nonprofits.

WHAT KIND OF HELP CAN EXTERNAL PROVIDERS OFFER?

Capacity-building providers can assist in training, peer exchanges, convening, and consulting or, even better, through a combination of these.

TRAINING

Training and educational opportunities primarily enhance technical capacity since they enable employees, directors, and volunteers to develop the necessary skills to do a better job of managing, overseeing, and performing the work of their organization. Offerings can range from brief seminars to yearlong, university-based courses. Whatever the format, adults learn best when there is a clear agenda with specific goals and when there is an opportunity to apply new skills and concepts to real-life work situations.

---

34. Parts of this chapter were adapted from *Strengthening Nonprofit Performance: A Funder's Guide to Capacity Building* by Paul Connolly and Carol Lukas.

Peer Exchange

Peer exchanges — including roundtables, case-study groups, and learning circles — are based on the premise that participants can be both teachers and learners. To be most successful, peer exchanges need a skilled facilitator, a safe environment in which participants can express and modify their beliefs, and a balance of structure and flexibility. Peer exchanges can lessen the isolation of participants, help them become more self-confident, and heighten their awareness of diverse views and alternate solutions. These exchanges can enhance leadership capacity when peer chief executives or board members are involved.

Convening

When nonprofit board members and chief executives from different organizations gather together in one setting, each can improve his or her adaptive capacity by learning from each other, sharing resources, and planning collaborations. By marshalling their forces together, nonprofits have considerable power to influence funding trends, complex community issues, or developmental challenges. Banding together can facilitate joint action.

Consulting

Consulting is a broad term that describes a wide array of relationships between a nonprofit client and a professional advisor, whether an independent consultant, nonprofit management-support organization, or private consulting firm. Consulting roles vary depending on the consultant's style and background, the needs of the client, and the type of project. Therefore, depending on the nature of the engagement, consulting can help strengthen any of the four core capacities. In some cases, a consultant acts primarily as a directive expert, conveying information and prescribing solutions related to programs, organizational development, or specialized areas such as accounting or fundraising. In other situations, a consultant plays the role of a facilitator, guiding a process and collaboratively helping the client to reflect on options and make decisions. Consulting engagements are most successful when the advisor and client agree upon goals and strategies, have clear mutual expectations, share a commitment to making change, and dedicate adequate time to the effort. Consultants often can also provide staff with the skills to perpetuate the consultant's work after the engagement ends.

Communicating with Funders

At each phase of a nonprofit's evolution, an organization can seek help from funders to fortify its core capacities, move its capacities into alignment, navigate transitions, advance to the next stage of development, and sustain itself. Most funder strategies involve providing financial resources through grants and loans, but a funder can also provide direct management assistance or focus on supporting outside capacity builders and intermediaries, who in turn provide benefits to a nonprofit.

How can a nonprofit best convince grantmakers to help build its capacities? In general, it should be stressed to funders that strong organizations lead to strong programs, and that an organization is far more likely to achieve its programmatic goals if it is also well managed. Many of the commonly understood methods of strengthening program effectiveness and reach — evaluating and redesigning programs, bringing successful pilot efforts to scale, spurring replication, and furthering in-depth partnerships and collaborations — require capacity building, just as a growing private company requires working capital.

Investing in capacity building is an effective way for a funder to leverage its philanthropic resources and multiply its impact. Writing in the *Harvard Business Review*, Michael Porter and Mark Kramer explain: "By helping grantees to improve their own capabilities, foundations can affect the social productivity of more resources than just their slice of the whole." Porter and Kramer point out that "foundations can create still more value if they move beyond the role of capital provider to the role of fully engaged partner, thereby improving the grantee's effectiveness as an organization."[35] This is an important reminder when making the case to a funder.

A proposal should also make clear to grantmakers that capacity building has long been an integral aspect of for-profit business practices. Private-sector investors look for corporations that have excellent and involved leadership, adaptive capacity, good management systems, and sound infrastructure. Yet historically, most investors in the nonprofit sector — i.e., funders and grantors — have focused almost exclusively on programmatic work and front-end programs. Even worse, grantmakers have sometimes created disincentives to good management by emphasizing new programs and short-term results at the expense of a nonprofit's infrastructure and mission.

KNOWING WHAT TO ASK FOR

As discussed in previous chapters, capacity-building needs are unique to each stage of the nonprofit lifecycle. There are typically three main areas in which grantmakers provide help to nonprofits with such needs: management assistance, grants, and capital financing. It is important for those making the ask to be familiar with these three areas in order to make a strong case as to why grantors should invest in capacity building. (See Appendix 3 for a detailed list of types of capacity-building support to seek from grantmakers at each stage of the lifecycle.)

Management Assistance

A funder can enhance nonprofit organizational effectiveness by supporting groups that provide capacity-building assistance to nonprofits, including nonprofit management and training providers, intermediaries, independent consultants, and private consulting firms. Grantmakers sometimes refer a nonprofit to those service providers, and either subsidize a grantee's retention of their services or contract directly with providers to assist a nonprofit. A small but growing group of funders, some of which self-identify as "venture philanthropists," is providing its own staff assistance directly to nonprofits.

Grants

Some funders are now incorporating capacity building into their regular grantmaking process. Many of those grantmakers solicit and award grants to nonprofits specifically to build organizational capacity through such activities as strategic planning, board development, or staff training. A funder may accomplish the same goal more indirectly by

---

35. Porter, Michael E. and Mark R. Kramer. "Philanthropy's New Agenda: Creating Value." *Harvard Business Review*. November-December 1999.

considering organizational growth issues when reviewing proposals, liberalizing rules on indirect costs, and funding management assistance as a component of a program grant. Targeted funding for general operations can also provide impetus for increasing organizational effectiveness. General operating support can enable a group to invest in much needed infrastructure — such as technology, administrative staff, and operational systems — that are not usually covered by project and program funding. Funders may provide general-support grants that are proportional to a grantee's overall budget (10-20 percent), and link them to a nonprofit's meeting the goals in its strategic plan.

Capital Financing

Capital financing is another way a funder can help a nonprofit improve its financial position, institute healthy financial practices, improve productivity and performance, and progress to another lifecycle stage. There are three types of capital: facilities capital, working capital, and permanent capital.[36] Facilities capital supports the renovation, building, or acquisition of office and program space. Working capital helps a nonprofit cover expenses during times of low cash flow and provides it with unrestricted cash, enabling it to build capacity. Permanent capital refers to endowment funding or to the capital reserves that some nonprofit organizations invest in areas such as housing and business development. Capital financing is usually provided in the form of loans at below-market rates, or sometimes by outright grant.

Improving capacity is a time-consuming and complicated process at every stage of the nonprofit lifecycle. When staff members and/or board members seek funding for capacity building, they should gently remind funders to avoid creating inflated expectations for positive results over a short time period. Everyone involved in the capacity-building effort should understand that change takes hard work and time, but it is important for nonprofit leaders to both anticipate funders' eagerness to see results and communicate with the funders or grantees on a regular basis so that capacity building doesn't become unrealistic within the designated timeframe.

QUESTIONS FOR THE BOARD AND THE CHIEF EXECUTIVE

- Does your organization need outside capacity-building support through training, peer exchange, convening, or consulting? If so, what type of help would be beneficial and why? How will you identify possible providers?

- What is the best way for your nonprofit to make the case for capacity-building support from a funder?

- What type of support (management assistance, grants, capital financing) does your organization need? How can this support be best tailored to your nonprofit's developmental stage?

- Which funders are the best prospects for your nonprofit to seek capacity-building support from?

---

36. Ryan, William. *Nonprofit Capital: A Review of Problems and Strategies.* New York and Washington, DC: Rockefeller Foundation and Fannie Mae Foundation, 2001.

Conclusion

The work of improving the performance of a nonprofit organization is difficult and complex — there is no single right way to do it and no predetermined timeframe for completing it. But, as discussed, there are frameworks and approaches that can help make the effort more effective.

Understanding where an organization falls in its cycle of development and how to build capacity along the way is an effort that must be made: As leaders of a nonprofit, board members and executive staff must work together to articulate a vision for the organization at every stage of the nonprofit's life and find the best ways make it a reality. In an era of increased scrutiny by the public and government agencies, this mandate has taken on even more urgency for nonprofits.

Psychologist and philosopher William James noted, "human beings, by changing the inner attitudes of their minds, can change the outer aspects of their lives." By better understanding the stages of a nonprofit's lifecycle and the important capacities necessary to sustain it, board members and executives can do the same for a nonprofit organization. In every phase, nonprofits are faced with new challenges. Why does a decrease in demand for a service or a funding cutback lead one nonprofit to adapt and thrive and another to die? According to Grantmakers for Effective Organizations, it is "the ability of an organization to fulfill its mission through a blend of sound management, strong governance, and a persistent rededication to achieving results."[37]

After reading this book, take the opportunity to step back and reflect on the passages and paragraphs that have particular resonance for the nonprofit you associate with. Open a dialogue with fellow board members or senior staff. Talk to the leaders of other nonprofits that have successfully — or unsuccessfully — managed transitions. All it takes is one leader to begin the process that can bring transformative change.

---

37. Grantmakers Evaluation Network and Grantmakers for Effective Organizations. "High Performance Organizations: Linking Evaluation and Effectiveness." *Report from 2000 GEN-GEO Conference*. Kansas City, MO: March, 2000.

Appendix 1

INDICATORS FOR HIGH-PERFORMING NONPROFIT ORGANIZATIONS

TCC Group, using an assessment tool based on the organizational capacity model described in this book, identified some specific organizational proficiencies that high-performing nonprofits have in common. Performance indicators derived from this preliminary research are described for each core capacity below.[38]

ADAPTIVE CAPACITY

Definition: The ability of a nonprofit organization to monitor, assess, respond to, and stimulate internal and external changes.

Performance Indicators

- *Environmental Learning*: how well an organization collaborates and networks with constituents, community leaders, and funders to learn about what's going on in the community and field.

- *Organizational Learning and Planning*: how well an organization assesses itself and uses assessment findings to conduct strategic planning and follow through on strategic plans.

- *Programmatic Learning*: how well an organization assesses the needs of its clients and conducts and uses program evaluation as a learning tool.

- *Decision-Making Tools*: how well an organization uses tools and resources to make decisions, such as staff and client input, outside management assistance, and/or a written strategic plan.

- *New Resource Acquisition*: how well an organization partners with funders, other non-profit organizations, and community leaders to secure resources that best serve the mission.

- *Organizational Sustainability*: the extent to which an organization has diverse and stable revenue streams and is not overly reliant on a few funders.

- *Program Sustainability*: whether an organization has sufficient financial resources to support programs on an ongoing basis, and how well an organization can adjust its programs to changes in funding.

How To Build: Needs assessment, organizational assessment, program evaluation, knowledge management, planning, and collaborations and partnerships

---

38. These indicators are derived from research that TCC Group conducted for The Pfizer Foundation in 2004.

LEADERSHIP CAPACITY

Definition: The ability of staff and board leaders to inspire, prioritize, make decisions, provide direction, and innovate, all in an effort to achieve the organizational mission.

Performance Indicators

- *Board Leadership*: how well a board performs with respect to holding organizational executive staff accountable for the mission and vision, conducting community outreach to educate funders and other supporters and garner resources, providing fiscal oversight, and performing other board functions.

- *Executive Leadership*: how well staff leaders communicate and engender the organizational mission and vision with other staff, the quality of the decision-making process within the organization, how flexible and open staff leaders are to engaging others in decision making, and how well executive leaders motivate staff.

- *Board-to-Executive Relationship*: the frequency and quality of interactions between board members and executive staff.

- *Leader Influence*: how well organizational leaders can persuade other board and staff, as well as community leaders and decision makers, to take action.

- *Community Leadership and Credibility*: how well an organization is perceived by the community to be a respected leader that represents and communicates well with the community.

- *Leadership Sustainability*: the degree to which an organization is not too reliant on one leader and has a succession plan.

How To Build: Board development, executive leadership development, and leadership transitions

MANAGEMENT CAPACITY

Definition: The ability of a nonprofit organization to ensure the effective and efficient use of organizational resources.

Performance Indicators

- *Staff Development*: how well staff managers recruit, coach, mentor, train, and empower staff to improve their skills and innovate.

- *Supporting Staff Resource Needs*: how well managers provide capable resources, tools, systems, and people needed to carry out the work.

- *Program Staffing*: how well managers are able to make staffing changes to increase and/or improve programs and service delivery.

- *Managing Program Staff Performance*: how well organizational managers ensure that program staff has the knowledge, skills, and cultural sensitivity to effectively deliver services.

- *Managing All Staff Performance*: how well an organization ensures that staff members are clear about their roles and responsibilities and are provided with frequent and regular constructive feedback.

- *Conveying Value of Staff*: how well managers provide positive feedback, rewards, and time for reflection to its staff.

- *Assessing Staff Performance*: how well managers assess staff performance and how well staff understands performance assessment criteria.

- *Problem Solving*: how effectively, judiciously, and consistently organizational managers resolve human resource problems and interpersonal conflicts, including how well they engage staff in the problem-solving process.

- *Volunteer Management*: how well staff members recruit, retain, direct, develop, value, and reward volunteers.

- *Manager-to-Staff Communication*: how clear the channels of communication are between managers and staff, as well as how open managers are to constructive feedback.

- *Financial Management*: how well organizational finances are managed.

How To Build: Human-resource development and management, internal communications, and financial management

TECHNICAL CAPACITY

Definition: The ability of a nonprofit organization to implement all of the key organizational functions and deliver programs and services.

Performance Indicators

- *Service Delivery Skills* to ensure efficient and quality services.

- *Evaluation Skills* to conduct research to effectively evaluate program delivery and client outcomes.

- *Outreach and Advocacy Skills* for outreach, organizing, and advocacy.

- *Marketing and Communications Skills* to effectively market to and communicate with internal and external stakeholders.

- *Legal Skills* to follow the law and effectively handle legal matters.

- *Fundraising Skills* to develop the necessary contributed resources for efficient and effective operations.

- *Earned Income Generation Skills* to generate earned revenues.

- *Accounting Skills* to ensure efficient and sound operations.

- *Facilities Management Skills* to ensure efficient and effective operations.

- *Technology Skills* to ensure efficient and effective operations.

How To Build: Increase skills in service delivery, evaluation, outreach and advocacy, marketing and communications, legal, fundraising, earned income generation, accounting, facilities management, and technology

Appendix 2

NONPROFIT ORGANIZATIONAL LIFECYCLE ASSESSMENT TOOL

Part 1 of this assessment tool is designed to summarize in an easy-to-use chart form the essential capacities necessary at each stage of the nonprofit lifecycle. It can help focus on which developmental stage or stages your nonprofit is currently passing through and whether its current capacities are sufficient to sustain it at that stage. This tool can complement organizational assessment instruments that entail quantitative analysis.

Space is provided below each capacity summary for your own assessment and comments. It is a useful instrument at any time, but particularly when an organization is undertaking an organizational assessment or strategic planning process.

Invite senior staff members and board leaders to independently fill out the assessment form; then use the questions in Part 2 to discuss the differences and similarities among their answers. This will likely stir a lively and informative debate that could be the first step to real change and improvement in the organization.

Parts 1 and 2 of this assessment can also be found on the CD-ROM attached to the back of this book. The electronic version may be used for customization purposes and ease of distribution.

PART 1: NONPROFIT ORGANIZATIONAL LIFECYCLE ASSESSMENT GRID

	START-UP (to begin)	ADOLESCENT (to grow)	MATURE (to sustain)	STAGNANT (to renew)	DEFUNCT (to dissolve)
ADAPTIVE CAPACITY					
Needs Assessment	· Organization has informal, hands-on ways to identify constituent needs, such as by talking extensively to a network of community leaders and potential clients.	· Organization develops moderately broad and deep connections with community leaders, funders, and constituents and learns about needs through these relationships. · Organization conducts moderately comprehensive needs assessment using some market research methods.	· Organization establishes very broad and deep connections with community leaders, funders, and constituents and learns about changing needs through these relationships. · Organization conducts comprehensive needs assessments using market research methods.	· Organization re-establishes connections among community leaders, funders, and constituents and reassesses needs among constituents. · Organization conducts comprehensive needs assessments using market research methods.	· Organization assesses needs of remaining clients and refers them to other programs and discusses the possibility of handing off any residual programs to other organizations.
Check box that best fits your organization:					
Comments on rationale for choice and how much this matters:					
Organizational Assessment	· Organizational leaders have periodic reflective conversations about how the organization is performing and identifies basic ways to improve the management and governance of the organization.	· Organization undertakes a formal self-assessment process annually (perhaps using an organizational self-assessment instrument), identifies needs for improving the management and governance of the organization, and incorporates this thinking into a strategic planning process.	· On an ongoing basis, organization assesses itself (perhaps using an outside consultant to facilitate the process), identifies comprehensive needs for improving the management and governance of the organization, and incorporates this thinking into a strategic planning process.	· Organization candidly assesses itself, recognizes the need for organizational renewal, identifies critical areas for organizational improvement, and incorporates this thinking into a renewal process.	· Organization assesses itself and recognizes that it needs to shut down. · Organization identifies resources, assets, and programs that other non-profits in the community might be able to use or acquire.
Check box that best fits your organization:					
Comments on rationale for choice and how much this matters:					

	START-UP (to begin)	ADOLESCENT (to grow)	MATURE (to sustain)	STAGNANT (to renew)	DEFUNCT (to dissolve)
ADAPTIVE CAPACITY					
Program Evaluation	· Program volunteers and staff have periodic reflective discussions about what seems to be working with the programs and why, and keep track of anecdotes and stories that relate to outcomes.	· Program staff develop simple systems for gathering and using data about programmatic outcomes.	· Organization develops formal system for regularly evaluating programs. · Program model is documented so that it becomes more transferable.	· Organization conducts program evaluation and uses the results to inform and revise programs as part of renewal effort.	· Organization stops investing in program evaluation, documents what it has learned, and shares this information with key constituents. · Organization shares evaluation tools and processes with other non-profits in the community.
Check box that best fits your organization:					
Comments on rationale for choice and how much this matters:					
Knowledge Management	· Staff and board have periodic reflective conversations about what was learned during informal needs assessment, organizational assessment, program evaluation, and other sources, and how it relates to possible organizational improvements. · Organization develops simple systems for storing, organizing, disseminating, and using its knowledge.	· Staff and board develop simple systems for integrating and using data from needs assessment, organizational assessment, program evaluation, and other sources and how it relates to organizational improvements. · Organization develops simple systems for storing, organizing, disseminating, and using its knowledge.	· Staff and board develop formal systems for integrating and using data from needs assessment, organizational assessment, program evaluation, and other sources, and how it relates to organizational improvement.	· Staff and board revamp and improve systems for integrating and using data from needs assessment, organizational assessment, program evaluation, and other sources, and relating it to the organizational renewal effort.	· Organization reflects on what it has learned and shares this information with key constituents.
Check box that best fits your organization:					
Comments on rationale for choice and how much this matters:					

ADAPTIVE CAPACITY

	START-UP (to begin)	ADOLESCENT (to grow)	MATURE (to sustain)	STAGNANT (to renew)	DEFUNCT (to dissolve)
Strategic Planning	· Organizational leaders create a strategic thinking piece with a 2-year horizon that explains how it will start up the organization. · Organization has a simple plan for generating revenues from at least one major funding source.	· Organization articulates a clear theory of change. · Organization creates a strategic plan with a 3-5-year horizon that has clear goals and annual objectives, and develops annual operating plans and program plans based on it. · Organization has a plan for generating revenues from at least two or three main sources to enable the organization to grow.	· Organization creates a detailed updated theory of change. · Organization creates a strategic plan with a 3-5 year horizon that has clear goals and annual objectives, and develops annual operating plans and program plans based on it. · Organization has a plan for securing diverse and stable revenue sources, possibly including business plans for earned income and fundraising campaigns for capital projects. · Organization considers developing or creates a plan to develop a cash reserve or endowment.	· Organization affirms or revises a theory of change. · Organization creates a turnaround plan that has clear goals and objectives and creates an annual operating plan based on it. · Organization has a plan for restoring the confidence of dedicated funders and enlisting the support of new ones so that the organization stabilizes financially.	· Organization creates a plan to dissolve itself in a responsible and orderly manner.
Check box that best fits your organization:					
Comments on rationale for choice and how much this matters:					

	START-UP (to begin)	ADOLESCENT (to grow)	MATURE (to sustain)	STAGNANT (to renew)	DEFUNCT (to dissolve)		
ADAPTIVE CAPACITY							
Collaborations and Partnerships	· Organization forms relationships with other groups and begins informally cooperating with some of them, such as by sharing information and making cross-referrals.	· Organization develops connections with other organizations and forges more formal collaborations with some of them, such as by coordinating program delivery and sharing resources.	· Organization develops strong connections with other organizations and considers developing or does develop such formal collaborations as joint ventures or shared back-office space and functions.	· Organization maintains relationships with other organizations, develops new relationships, and considers collaborations and partnerships as a part of its renewal effort.	· Organization ends any collaborations with other organizations and considers handing off some programs to other groups and referring clients to them. · Organization meets with other nonprofit leaders and funders to discuss ways to address client needs in an ongoing manner.		
Check box that best fits your organization:							
Comments on rationale for choice and how much this matters:							

LEADERSHIP CAPACITY

	START-UP (to begin)	ADOLESCENT (to grow)	MATURE (to sustain)	STAGNANT (to renew)	DEFUNCT (to dissolve)
Board Development	· Organization establishes a small homogenous board. · Board develops a clear purpose and vision that is understood by itself, staff, and volunteers. · Board plays a hands-on role in overseeing and managing the organization. · Board conducts an informal performance review of the chief executive.	· Organization expands the size of the board. · Board's role is formalized and there are job descriptions for board members. · Board articulates a clear mission, vision, and set of values and they are well understood by board, staff, and volunteers. · Board clarifies its role in relation to chief executive, increases its planning function, and develops a deliberate decision-making process. · Board conducts a formal annual evaluation of the chief executive and talks about a succession plan. · Board discusses how it is performing and how it needs to improve.	· Organization has a formal nominating process and adds people to the board who represent the community that the organization serves and have skills that the organization requires, such as program, financial, and legal expertise. · Organization affirms or revises its mission, vision, and values, and they are well understood by board, staff, and volunteers. · Board clarifies its role in relation to the chief executive, reduces its operational role, and increases its policy and fundraising function. · Board has committees, work groups, or task forces and, possibly, advisory committees. · Board conducts a formal annual evaluation of the chief executive and creates a succession plan. · Board formally assesses itself and creates a board development plan.	· Organization retires some veteran board members who are not engaged and adds new board members who support the renewal effort. · Organization affirms or revises its mission, vision, and values, and they are well understood by board, staff, and volunteers. · The board plays a hands-on role during the renewal effort and ensures the financial viability of the organization. · The board reviews the performance of the chief executive and, if necessary, terminates the person and hires a new one to lead the renewal effort.	· Board ensures that the organization's dissolution process is responsible and orderly. · Board dissolves itself.
Check box that best fits your organization:					
Comments on rationale for choice and how much this matters:					

LEADERSHIP CAPACITY

	START-UP (to begin)	ADOLESCENT (to grow)	MATURE (to sustain)	STAGNANT (to renew)	DEFUNCT (to dissolve)
Executive Leadership Development	· Volunteer or staff person founds organization or board hires staff leader. · Staff leader is entrepreneurial and adept at establishing and growing the organization.	· Chief executive's role is distinct in relation to the board. · Chief executive disconnects personal and organizational needs as the organization ages and expands. · Chief executive has the ability to manage the growth of the organization.	· The chief executive and board have distinct roles and they hold each other accountable. · Chief executive is adept at managing a large staff and complex finances and sustaining the organization. · Chief executive forms a strong senior management team, including possibly a chief operating officer.	· Chief executive is adept at managing a turnaround process.	· Chief executive completes his or her duties and leaves the organization.
Check box that best fits your organization:					
Comments on rationale for choice and how much this matters:					
Leadership Transitions	· Board hires chief executive. · Board appoints board chair.	· Board ensures that chief executive has the ability to manage the growth of the organization, and, if necessary, hires a new chief executive who is more able to do so. · Succession plans exist for staff and board leadership.	· Board ensures that chief executive has the ability to sustain the organization and, if necessary, hires a new chief executive who is more able to do so. · Succession plans exist for executive and staff leadership.	· Board determines if chief executive is able to renew the organization and, if necessary, hires a new chief executive who is more able to do so.	· Chief executive leaves job and board dissolves itself in an orderly manner.
Check box that best fits your organization:					
Comments on rationale for choice and how much this matters:					

	START-UP (to begin)	ADOLESCENT (to grow)	MATURE (to sustain)	STAGNANT (to renew)	DEFUNCT (to dissolve)
MANAGEMENT CAPACITY					
Human-Resource Development and Management	· Organization has a small number of volunteers or staff and there is little or no organizational hierarchy. · Organizational leaders establish roles for staff and volunteers and recruit and hire people. · Volunteers and staff are informally oriented, trained, and evaluated. · Staff decision-making process is informal. · There are few or no formal personnel policies.	· Organizational leaders develop recruitment and hiring plan, write job descriptions for volunteers and staff, recruit and hire them, and establish a simple organizational hierarchy. · Staff orientation and training becomes more formal, and annual staff evaluations are established. · Staff decision-making process becomes more formal. · Simple personnel policies are established.	· Organization hires additional staff, including program specialists and professional managers, and creates a more centralized and hierarchical organizational structure that has a clear division of labor and reporting relationships. · Organization has a formal staff orientation, training, and evaluation process. · Well-developed personnel policies exist.	· Organizational leaders revise staff job descriptions and restructure staff to reflect plan to renew the organization.	· Organizational leaders terminate staff respectfully.
Check box that best fits your organization:					
Comments on rationale for choice and how much this matters:					
Internal Communications	· Organization communicates informally among staff, such as by having sporadic conversations and meetings.	· Organization develops more formal methods for communicating, such as by holding regular staff meetings and documenting and disseminating what is discussed at them.	· Organization has formal methods for communicating among staff, such as by having a management reporting system, staff meetings at the departmental and organizational levels, and a regular staff newsletter.	· Organizational leaders freely share information with all staff about the organizational renewal efforts.	· Organizational leaders clearly communicate with staff about dissolution plans.
Check box that best fits your organization:					
Comments on rationale for choice and how much this matters:					

MANAGEMENT CAPACITY

	START-UP (to begin)	ADOLESCENT (to grow)	MATURE (to sustain)	STAGNANT (to renew)	DEFUNCT (to dissolve)
Financial Management	· Organizational leaders create a basic annual budget and meet regularly to discuss how to allocate financial resources. · Organization establishes a basic accounting system, which may be cash-based, and creates annual financial statements that are audited internally and approved by the board. · Organization has adequate human resources, such as a part-time bookkeeper, to handle the financial management function.	· Organizational leaders create a multiyear budget and meet regularly to discuss how to allocate financial resources, manage cash flow, and live within its means. · Organization develops an accrual accounting system and creates quarterly financial reports (which show budget vs. actual figures) and an annual financial statement that is audited by an outside Certified Public Accountant and approved by the board. · Organization has adequate human resources, such as a full-time financial manager, to handle the financial management function.	· Organizational leaders create a multiyear budget and discuss how to allocate financial resources and live within its means. · Organization maintains a well-developed accrual accounting system, creates quarterly financial reports that include projections, and produces an annual financial statement that is audited by an outside Certified Public Accountant and approved the board. · Organization creates monthly cash flow projections and manages its cash flow well. · If necessary, organization has ability to manage a capital budget, cash reserve, and/or an endowment. · Organization has adequate human resources, such as a chief financial officer or comptroller, to handle the financial management function.	· Organizational leaders assess the financial situation frequently, strengthen financial controls, and ensure that the organization is living within its means. · Organization continues to maintain a well-developed accrual accounting system and creates quarterly financial reports and annual audited financial statements. · Organization has adequate human resources to handle the financial management function during the renewal effort and may need to hire a new staff person to handle the financial management function and/or replace the outside auditor.	· Organizational leaders distribute any remaining assets and fulfill any outstanding financial obligations.
Check box that best fits your organization:					
Comments on rationale for choice and how much this matters:					

TECHNICAL CAPACITY

	START-UP (to begin)	ADOLESCENT (to grow)	MATURE (to sustain)	STAGNANT (to renew)	DEFUNCT (to dissolve)
Service Delivery Skills	· Organization establishes basic skills to effectively provide simple programs that meet the needs that it identifies.	· Organization has skills to expand responsive and credible programs that respond to changing needs and maintain their quality.	· Organization has skills to refine comprehensive programs based on changing needs.	· Organization has skills to revise programs to be responsive to needs as part of organizational renewal effort.	· Organization has skills to responsibly end programs and refer clients elsewhere.
Check box that best fits your organization:					
Comments on rationale for choice and how much this matters:					
Evaluation Skills	· Organization has fundamental skills to have reflective conversations about program outcomes and informally evaluate programs.	· Organization has skills to establish and implement simple systems for program evaluation.	· Organization has skills to evaluate programs regularly, systematically, and formally, and document the program model.	· Organization has skills to evaluate programs to inform decisions about program revisions.	· Organization has skills to document outcomes and lessons learned, and communicate this information to stakeholders.
Check box that best fits your organization:					
Comments on rationale for choice and how much this matters:					
Outreach and Advocacy Skills	· Organization builds basic skills to develop strong connections with constituents and effectively perform outreach and advocacy.	· Organization builds strong skills to develop and maintain solid connections with constituents, and effectively perform outreach and advocacy.	· Organization maintains and further improves skills to develop strong connections with constituents and effectively perform outreach and advocacy.	· Organization has skills to effectively maintain and develop strong connections with constituents, and revise outreach and advocacy efforts as part of organizational renewal effort.	· Organization has skills to responsibly end outreach and advocacy efforts.
Check box that best fits your organization:					
Comments on rationale for choice and how much this matters:					

	START-UP (to begin)	ADOLESCENT (to grow)	MATURE (to sustain)	STAGNANT (to renew)	DEFUNCT (to dissolve)
TECHNICAL CAPACITY					
Marketing and Communications Skills	· Organization has adequate ability to market its programs and services and communicate about its activities in simple ways, such as through word-of-mouth and written program descriptions.	· Organization has ability to market its programs and services and communicate about its activities in moderately advanced ways, such as by creating simple brochures.	· Organization has ability to market its programs and services and communicate about its activities in advanced ways, such as through a Web site, newsletter, and annual report.	· Organization has ability to market its revised programs and services and communicate honestly and clearly with constituents about the renewal effort.	· Organization has ability to communicate with stakeholders about its accomplishments and dissolution.
Check box that best fits your organization:					
Comments on rationale for choice and how much this matters:					
Legal Skills	· Organization has legal skills necessary for the organization, such as for creating bylaws and articles of incorporation and obtaining tax-exempt status.	· Organization has legal skills necessary for the organization, such as for employment, leases, and insurance.	· Organization has advanced legal skills necessary for the organization, such as for joint ventures, trademark and licensing issues, and construction contracts.	· Organization has legal skills necessary for the organization, such as for renegotiating debt with creditors, restructuring, or terminating contracts.	· Organization has access to basic legal skills necessary for the organization, such as for terminating leases and bankruptcy.
Check box that best fits your organization:					
Comments on rationale for choice and how much this matters:					

TECHNICAL CAPACITY

	START-UP (to begin)	ADOLESCENT (to grow)	MATURE (to sustain)	STAGNANT (to renew)	DEFUNCT (to dissolve)
Fundraising Skills	· Organization has skills to secure contributed revenue from at least one main source.	· Organization has skills to secure contributed revenues from several main sources.	· Organization has skills to secure contributed revenues from diverse sources and, if necessary, effectively conduct a capital campaign for a capital project, cash reserve, or endowment.	· Organization has skills to reassure current funders and maintain their support, and enlist new ones to support the renewal effort.	· Organization has skills to responsibly end relationships with funders and donors. · Organization has skills to broker relationships between other nonprofits working with the same clients and their funders in order to meet the ongoing needs of their clients.
Check box that best fits your organization:					
Comments on rationale for choice and how much this matters:					
Earned-Income Generation Skills	· Organization has skills to begin planning possible earned-income activities.	· Organization has skills to generate a limited amount of earned income.	· Organization has skills to generate a moderate to high amount of earned income.	· Organization has ability to maintain or increase any earned income during renewal effort.	· Organization has ability to responsibly end relationships with customers who generated earned income.
Check box that best fits your organization:					
Comments on rationale for choice and how much this matters:					

TECHNICAL CAPACITY

	START-UP (to begin)	ADOLESCENT (to grow)	MATURE (to sustain)	STAGNANT (to renew)	DEFUNCT (to dissolve)
Accounting Skills	· Organization has accounting and financial management skills needed to set up payroll, create and manage an annual budget, establish and implement a simple accounting system, and create annual financial statements.	· Organization has accounting and financial management skills to create and manage a multiyear budget, manage cash flow, implement a moderately advanced accrual accounting system, and create quarterly financial reports and annual audited financial statements.	· Organization has accounting and financial management skills to create and manage a multiyear budget, manage cash flow, implement an advanced accrual accounting system, create quarterly financial reports and annual audited financial statements, and, if necessary, manage a capital budget, cash reserve, and/or endowment.	· Organization has accounting and financial management skills to strengthen financial controls, manage a multiyear budget, manage cash flow, implement an advanced accrual accounting system, create quarterly financial reports and annual audited financial statements, and anything else required to support the organizational renewal effort.	· Organization has accounting and financial management skills to distribute any remaining assets and fulfill any outstanding financial obligations.
Check box that best fits your organization:					
Comments on rationale for choice and how much this matters:					
Facilities Management Skills	· Organization has fundamental skills to manage, operate, and maintain its facilities, such as borrowing, subleasing, leasing, and maintaining office and program space.	· Organization has skills to manage, operate, and maintain its facilities, such as by leasing and maintaining additional space for expanding programs.	· Organization has advanced skills to manage, operate, and maintain its facility, such as by purchasing, building, upgrading, leasing, and managing additional program and office space.	· Organization has skills to manage, operate, and maintain its facilities, such as by consolidating space, selling property, or subletting.	· Organization has basic skills to manage its facilities, such as by terminating leases and selling property.
Check box that best fits your organization:					
Comments on rationale for choice and how much this matters:					

	START-UP (to begin)	ADOLESCENT (to grow)	MATURE (to sustain)	STAGNANT (to renew)	DEFUNCT (to dissolve)
TECHNICAL CAPACITY					
Technology Skills	· Organization has basic skills to use and manage technology, such as telephone, fax, and computer hardware and software.	· Organization has moderately advanced skills to use and manage technology, such as telephone, fax, a networked computer system, and basic applications.	· Organization has advanced skills to use and manage technology, including telephone, fax, a networked computer system, and a wide array of sophisticated applications.	· Organization has skills to use and manage technology to support the organization's renewal efforts.	· Organization has skills to shut down and end any technological systems that the organization has used.
Check box that best fits your organization:					
Comments on rationale for choice and how much this matters:					

PART 2: QUESTIONS ABOUT YOUR ORGANIZATIONAL LIFECYCLE ASSESSMENT

After you compile the results of the table above, discuss the findings among your board and staff. In particular, answer and discuss the following questions:

1. Overall, based on a review of your checks in each column, which stage best describes your organization now? Do you have characteristics distributed fairly equally in more than one stage? If so, what are these stages?

2. Does your organization want to evolve into another stage? If so, which one and when? If you want to remain in your current stage, explain why.

3. Given the overall stage your organization is trying to reach, how do you need to strengthen your adaptive capacity to help get there?

4. Given the overall stage your organization is trying to reach, how do you need to strengthen your leadership capacity to help get there?

5. Given the overall stage your organization is trying to reach, how do you need to strengthen your management capacity to help get there?

6. Given the overall stage your organization is trying to reach, how do you need to strengthen your technical capacity to help get there?

7. Which core capacities does your organization most need and want to strengthen to enhance your organizational effectiveness? How do you need to align the four core capacities better?

8. What are the capacity-building activities that are the highest priority for your organization to focus on over the next few years?

Appendix 3

TYPES OF CAPACITY-BUILDING SUPPORT TO SEEK FROM GRANTMAKERS AT EACH STAGE OF THE NONPROFIT LIFECYCLE

Capacity-building needs are unique to each stage of the nonprofit lifecycle. The information below outlines the kinds of capacity building that may be useful at each stage. For nonprofit grantseekers, it provides a menu of ideas to ask for support from funders through management assistance, grants, and capital financing to building capacity. An organization's particular proposal to a funder should be tailored to fit the nonprofit's needs and the funder's interests.

START-UP ORGANIZATIONS

Management Assistance

- Consulting, coaching, peer exchange, and training to help the nonprofit address challenges and tap the potential associated with the start-up phase, such as:

    - assessing needs among constituents

    - creating a brief strategic guide for the next year or two

    - enabling the executive leader to hire and manage staff well and set up simple human-resource management systems

    - establishing a board, articles of incorporation, and bylaws

    - creating a basic budget process and accounting system

    - developing a plan for generating revenue

- Referrals to capacity-building resources, such as Web sites, workshops, consultants, executive coaches, and other nonprofits that have successfully made their way through the start-up period.

Grants

- A program grant that considers programmatic potential and addresses the start-up's organizational capacity-building needs.

- A grant to support the types of capacity-building activities described in the "Management Assistance" section above, whether they are done by the nonprofit itself, or with the assistance of a consultant capacity builder.

- A general-operating support grant to enable the nonprofit to hire staff, rent space, set up basic management systems, and establish its administrative infrastructure.

Capital Financing

- An initial working capital loan to allow the nonprofit to originate and ramp up operations, based on a basic plan that shows how the nonprofit intends to use the capital, generate revenues, and pay back the loan.

ADOLESCENT ORGANIZATIONS

Management Assistance

- Consulting, coaching, peer exchange, and training to enable the nonprofit to grow through the changes in the adolescent stage and advance organizationally, including:

  - conducting an in-depth assessment of community or field needs

  - cultivating the staff leader's connection with other nonprofit leaders, and nurturing his or her management skills and ability to receive encouragement and support

  - performing a comprehensive organizational assessment

  - setting up a more formal knowledge-management system

  - creating a strategic plan for the organization to grow over the next 5-10 years

  - articulating a theory of change that informs program design and establishing formal systems for program evaluation

  - fortifying the human-resource management function, such as by instituting a formal orientation program or performance-assessment system

  - fostering a board development plan that spells out board roles and responsibilities, needed changes in the composition of the board, and modifications to its structure

  - devising a succession plan for the chief executive

  - developing a more sophisticated financial management system, especially for managing cash flow

  - creating a more detailed plan to generate diverse revenues

  - forging outside collaborations and partnerships

  - procuring the technology and facilities the organization needs to expand

- Referrals to other funders that might support the organization's maturation, to nonprofits that have planned and managed adolescent growth well, and to other capacity-building resources.

- Opportunities to receive mentoring from adolescent or mature nonprofits with proven capabilities in an area where the nonprofit needs and wants to improve.

Grants

- A program grant based on an emerging programmatic track record is conducive to the particular management and governance needs of a growing nonprofit, and may include matching requirements to provide an incentive to increase and diversify revenues.

- A grant to facilitate the capacity-building efforts listed above, which could be undertaken by the nonprofit on its own or with outside assistance.

- A general operating-support grant that enables the nonprofit to expand and is connected to its performance on a strategic plan.

Capital Financing

- A loan that helps the nonprofit cover expenses during times of low cash flow or provides it with unrestricted, flexible working capital to enable it to grow, such as by enhancing technology or starting an earned-income venture.

- A loan to support the renovation, building, or acquisition of office or program space.

MATURE ORGANIZATIONS

Management Assistance

- Consulting, coaching, peer exchange, and training to enable the nonprofit to maintain itself in a healthy maturity, such as:

  - affirming or revising its mission

  - undertaking a comprehensive organizational assessment that allows it to identify capacity-building priorities

  - updating the strategic plan and creating business plans for particular program areas and earned-income ventures

  - revisiting and possibly amending its theory of change and conducting ongoing program evaluation

  - refining human-resource management functions and formalizing systems for internal communications and staff-performance assessment

  - updating or creating a succession plan for the chief executive

  - revising the board-development plan

  - maintaining and continuing to improve the financial-management function

  - pursuing and enhancing partnerships and collaborations

  - enabling the chief executive to strengthen his or her leadership abilities

  - obtaining the technology and space the organization needs

  - enhancing the plan for generating diverse revenues

- Referrals to other funders and capacity builders that might help the nonprofit sustain itself in maturity.

- Referrals to other nonprofits that have remained relevant and vital in maturity over a period of time.

Grants

- A program grant that is contingent on documented positive program outcomes and that fosters the capacity of a mature nonprofit.

- A grant to support the nonprofit's or an outside capacity builder's efforts to strengthen the organization's performance, as outlined above.

- A major general-operating support grant provided as flexible unrestricted working capital for the nonprofit to become more pertinent and sustainable and that is linked to a nonprofit's strategic planning progress.

Capital Financing

- A loan for cash flow, working capital, or earned-income venture purposes.

- A loan to support the renovation, building, or acquisition of office or program space.

- A permanent capital grant, to enable a nonprofit to build an endowment or capital reserve, perhaps with a matching requirement that encourages the nonprofit to attract additional funding.

STAGNANT ORGANIZATIONS

Management Assistance

- Consulting, coaching, peer exchange, and training to allow the nonprofit to understand and overcome its deterioration, including activities related to:

  - increasing the awareness of the incipient stagnation and determining the feasibility of renewing the organization

  - performing market research to better understand changing market conditions

  - revamping systems for financial management and control

  - reviewing the performance of the current chief executive and possibly conducting a search to find a new one to lead a revival process

  - developing a turnaround plan that includes strategies for refocusing the organization's mission, revising programs, reorganizing staff, improving the board's performance, stabilizing finances, generating revenues, and restoring the confidence of stakeholders

- Referrals to grantmakers that might support a sound renewal plan.

- Opportunities to receive mentoring from other nonprofits that have successfully reinvigorated themselves.

Grants

- A program grant to support existing programs that are judged to be effective and possibly for new ones that have potential.

- A grant to cover costs associated with the assessment and turnaround activities indicated above.

- A general operating support grant that provides flexible support for reform efforts that is linked to the nonprofit's ability to implement its turnaround plan.

Capital Financing

- A loan to enable the organization to carry out the turnaround plan, which can be repaid after the organization renews itself and restabilizes.

DEFUNCT ORGANIZATIONS

Management Assistance

- Consulting, coaching, peer exchange, and training to assist the nonprofit to responsibly shut down, such as:

    - developing staff and client termination plans

    - referring clients to other programs and services

    - transferring effective programs to other nonprofits

    - documenting and disseminating lessons learned

    - communicating with constituents about the organization's demise

    - fulfilling all legal requirements associated with the organization's going out of business

    - meeting all financial obligations and distributing the remaining assets of the non-profit in accordance with law

- Facilitating the networking of high-quality staff with other nonprofits that may be hiring.

Grants

- A limited, final grant to support an orderly dissolution process or, when the process is disorderly, to pay for lawyers or other consultants to clean up the mess.

Suggested Resources

GENERAL RESOURCES

The resources below helped inform the writing of this book and can provide additional information on nonprofit organizational lifecycles and capacity building.

LIFECYCLES

Amherst H. Wilder Foundation. *Nonprofit Decline and Dissolution Project Report*. Saint Paul, MN: Amherst H. Wilder Foundation, 1989. This publication provides practical advice on how to dissolve a nonprofit organization in a responsible manner. It is a helpful guide for both staff and board members.

Arrick, Ellen and Anne MacKinnon. *Working with Start-Ups: Grantmakers and New Organizations*. New York: The Ford Foundation, Grantcraft, 2004. In this guide, grant makers from a wide range of funding organizations describe their experiences as supporters of new nonprofits. Find out how they negotiated the path from idea to organization, and what they learned along the way about how to solve problems and help an organization sustain itself into the future.

Connolly, Paul and Laura Colin Klein. "Getting in Shape: Fitness Tips for Established Nonprofits." *Nonprofit World*. January/February, 2000. Leaders of successful nonprofits make a practice of continually scanning the horizon for change, responding quickly to new challenges, and addressing internal problems. The authors give warning signs for organizations that may be on their way to decline, and add remedies for finding a successful turnaround.

Connolly, Paul and Laura Colin Klein. "Good Growth, Bad Growth, and How To Tell the Difference." *Nonprofit World*. May/June, 1999. Organizational growth is typically desirable, and nonprofit executives tend to talk about it in a positive light. The failure to grow or remain stable may lead to a decline in relevance and effectiveness — but not always. Connolly and Klein discuss risks in lack of planning and management in a growing organization, illustrating how bigger is not always better, and may turn out to be worse.

Grenier, Larry I. "Evolution and Revolution As Organizations Grow." *Harvard Business Review*. May, 1998. In this HBR Classic (originally published in 1972), Greiner identifies a series of developmental phases that companies tend to pass through as they grow. Each phase begins with a period of evolution, steady growth, and stability, and ends with a revolutionary period of organizational turmoil and change. The critical task for management is to find a new set of organizational practices as a basis for managing the next period of evolutionary growth. Greiner discusses managers' experience in the irony of seeing a major solution in one period become a major problem in a later period.

Hummel, Joan M. *Starting and Running a Nonprofit Organization*. Minneapolis, MN: University of Minnesota Press, 1996. This popular resource is for those who are forming new nonprofits; thinking about converting an informal, grassroots group into tax-exempt status; reorganizing an existing agency; or currently managing a nonprofit. It provides practical and basic how-to information on legal, tax, organizational, and other issues particular to nonprofits.

La Piana Associates, Inc. *Tool for Assessing Startup Organizations.* Washington DC: Grantmakers for Effective Organizations, 2003. Grantmakers have a responsibility as stewards of organizations' resources to assess the risk entailed in making grants to each nonprofit. This tool is designed for funders receiving grant applications from start-up nonprofits. It is designed to help program officers collect and think through the organization's strengths and weaknesses.

Management Assistance Group. "Steering Nonprofits: Advice for Board and Staff." *Historic Preservation Forum.* Washington, DC: National Trust for Historic Preservation, 1991. This article sums up the Management Assistance Group's views about how nonprofit organizations develop according to an organizational lifecycle. It includes advice about executive leadership transitions, shifting board roles, and changes in management systems and human resources.

Sharken Simon, Judith. *The 5 Life Stages of Nonprofit Organizations: Where You Are, Where You're Going, and What to Expect When You Get There.* St. Paul, MN: Amherst H. Wilder Foundation, 2001. This useful guide helps to understand where an organization is in its life. Readers will learn about the very real challenges and problems facing nonprofits at any given stage. Directors, board members, managers, and consultants can use this guide to: put problems in context, effectively manage transitions from one stage to the next, and watch for the warning signs of decline and dissolution. This book includes The Wilder Nonprofit Life Stage Assessment, which allows users to plot their organization's home stage and gauge its development.

Stevens Group, The. *Growing Up Nonprofit: An Essay on Nonprofit Life Cycle Development.* Minneapolis: The Stevens Group, 1993. This paper explains how nonprofit organizations develop along a lifecycle. It covers typical characteristics and challenges at each stage of organizational development and offers advice for managing transitions.

Stevens, Susan Kenny. *Nonprofit Lifecycles: Stage-Based Wisdom for Nonprofit Capacity.* Long Lake, MN: Stagewise Enterprises, 2002. This resource weighs in with a developmental perspective on nonprofit capacity and its relationship to increased organizational performance. Offering practical insights and thought-provoking case studies, this book presents seven nonprofit lifecycle stages and the predictable tasks, challenges, and inevitable growing pains that nonprofits encounter and can hope to master on the road to organizational sustainability.

CAPACITY BUILDING

Allison, Michael and Jude Kaye. *Strategic Planning for Nonprofit Organizations, Second Edition.* New York: John Wiley & Sons, Inc., 2005. This thoroughly revised, updated, and expanded edition arms you with the expert knowledge and tools you need to develop and implement surefire strategic plans, including tested-in-the-trenches worksheets, checklists, and tables, along with a book-length case study that lets you observe strategic planning in action.

Burns, Michael. "Act Your Age! The Organizational Lifecycle and How if Affects Your Board." *New England Nonprofit Quarterly.* Summer, 1997. Part of a four-part series of articles, this piece is based on the premise that boards, like the organizations they govern, grow in stages. What is best for one board in a certain stage of development may not be best for another in a different stage. It poses the question: "How does the environment in which the board works and organizational age of the board play a factor in their success or failure?"

Connolly, Paul and Carol Lukas. *Strengthening Nonprofit Performance: A Funder's Guide to Capacity Building*. Minneapolis, MN: Amherst H. Wilder Foundation, 2002. This book scans the many strategies that grantmakers can use to build the capacity of nonprofit organizations and communities, and provides examples of strategies employed by various grantmakers. The authors have organized the book for readers who want an overview of current thinking on capacity building and specific, how-to ideas about seven different capacity-building strategies that grantmakers can utilize.

Connolly, Paul and Peter York. *Building the Capacity of Capacity Builders: A Study of Management Support and Field-Building Organizations in the Nonprofit Sector.* New York: TCC Group, 2003. It is clear that capacity-building activities such as strategic planning, board development, and technology upgrades help enhance nonprofit organizational effectiveness. But the specific nature of the demand for capacity building, the quality and value of capacity-building services provided, and the health of the groups that provide this assistance are less clear. In this report, TCC Group strives to provide helpful insight into to the field of capacity building.

Connolly, Paul and Peter York. "Evaluating Capacity Building Efforts for Nonprofit Organizations." *OD Practitioner*. Vol. 34, No. 4, 2002. Growing numbers of grantmakers believe that investing in organizational capacity building helps leverage the impact of their philanthropic resources. In this article, Connolly and York explain how to evaluate capacity-building activities: determining who will conduct and participate in the evaluation; stating evaluation and potential success indicators and developing a framework for the evaluation design; implementing evaluation methods and using and sharing results.

Dart, Ray, Pat Bradshaw, Vic Murray, and Jacob Wolpin. "Boards of Directors in Nonprofit Organizations: Do They Follow a Lifecycle Model?" *Nonprofit Management & Leadership*. Summer, 1998. In this study, the authors used data from a survey of Canadian nonprofit organizations to empirically test hypotheses derived from models of nonprofit board life cycles. The authors suggest that while formal structural elements of board behavior change in the manner suggested by lifecycle models, the more enacted or behavioral aspects of nonprofit boards do not. The data further suggest caution in the use of lifecycle or age-dependent models to either explain or guide nonprofit board behavior.

Hernandez, Cynthia M. and Donald Leslie. "Charismatic Leadership: The Aftermath." *Nonprofit Management & Leadership*. Summer, 2001. This case study deals with the difficulties that may be encountered in the transition from a charismatic leader/founder to a more professionally focused chief executive in a human service organization. Resistance to change and obstacles confronting such an organizational change are explored.

Kibbe, Barbara and Fred Setterberg. *Succeeding With Consultants: Self-Assessment for the Changing Nonprofits*. New York: The Foundation Center, 1992. This book covers six different areas in which you might benefit from the advice of a consultant: governance, planning, fund development, financial management, public relations and marketing, and quality assurance.

Kotter, John P. *Leading Change*. Boston, MA: Harvard Business School Press, 1996. Kotter offers a practical approach to an organized means of leading, not managing, change. He presents an eight-stage process of change with highly useful examples that show how to go about implementing it. Based on experience with numerous companies, his sound advice gets directly at reasons that organizations fail to change — reasons that concern primarily the leader.

La Piana, David. *The Nonprofit Mergers Workbook: The Leader's Guide to Considering, Negotiating, and Executing a Merger*. St. Paul, MN: Amherst H. Wilder Foundation, 2000. This practical guide addresses why a merger is an important strategic tool for organizations focused on doing their best for their community. The text walks you through the entire merger process from assessing your reasons and readiness, to finding a partner, negotiating the deal, and completing the merger.

Letts, Christine W., William P. Ryan, and Allen Grossman. *High Performance Nonprofit Organizations: Managing Upstream for Greater Impact*. New York: John Wiley & Sons, 1999. Drawing on management techniques used by successful managers in both businesses and nonprofits, this book outlines approaches that nonprofits can use to build their capacity for learning, innovating, ensuring quality, and motivating staff. Illustrated with case studies and examples, the book outlines processes for achieving these goals, including: human-resource management, benchmarking, responsiveness and quality systems, and product development.

McKinsey & Company. *Effective Capacity Building in Nonprofit Organizations*. Washington, DC: Venture Philanthropy Partners, 2001. This report brings some common language to the discussion of capacity building and offers insights and examples of how nonprofits have pursued building up their organizational muscle. It contributes to the growing national conversation about how to help nonprofits become stronger, more sustainable, and better able to serve their communities. McKinsey also developed a practical assessment tool for this report that nonprofits can use to measure their own organizational capacity.

McLaughlin, Thomas. "Grewintos and Morphs: The Milestones of Spending." *Nonprofit Times*. September, 2003. This article explains how financial planning and management issues shift as a nonprofit organization grows and matures.

Oster, Sharon M. *Strategic Management for Nonprofit Organizations: Theory and Cases*. New York: Oxford University Press, 1995. This resource applies powerful concepts of strategic management developed originally in the for-profit sector to the management of nonprofits. It describes the preparation of a strategic plan consistent with the resources available; it analyzes the operational tasks in executing the plan; and describes the ways in which nonprofits need to change in order to remain competitive. The book draws clear distinctions between the different challenges encountered by nonprofits operating in different industries.

Sussman, Carl. "Making Change: How to Build Adaptive Capacity." *The Nonprofit Quarterly*. Winter, 2003. Sussman addresses the growing understanding of organizational performance through adaptive capacity, specifically. He explores internal capacity as well as external effectiveness, breaking down the four attributes of adaptive capacity: external focus, network connectedness, inquisitiveness, and innovation.

Wood, Miriam. "Is Governing Board Behavior Cyclical?" *Nonprofit Management and Leadership*. Winter, 2002. This article introduces an empirically driven model of cyclical board behavior, which holds that following a nonrecurring founding period, a board typically progresses through a sequence of three distinct operating phases and then experiences a crisis that initiates the whole sequence over again. During each cycle, board members become progressively less interested in the organization's mission and programs and more interested in the board's bureaucratic procedures and the organization's reputation for success in the community. Although the sequence of phases is predictable, the timing of them is not.

York, Peter. *Learning As We Go: Making Evaluation Work for Everyone*. New York: TCC Group, 2003. Through a concept termed "evaluative learning," York discusses the trend in which funders and nonprofit organizations are shifting away from using evaluation to prove the effectiveness of their work to others, toward enhancing what they do so they can achieve their mission and share successes with their peers inside and outside the organization.

GOVERNANCE PRACTICES

The resources below provide further guidance on specific board tasks and responsibilities that were discussed in the text. They are categorized according to what may be most appropriate for an organization during specific stages of its lifecycle, but all items in this list could be useful to organizations of all shapes and sizes.

START-UP

Grace, Kay Sprinkel. *The Nonprofit Board's Role in Setting and Advancing the Mission*. Washington, DC: BoardSource, 2003. Is your board actively supporting and advancing your organization's mission? Learn how board members can contribute to the creation of mission as well as communicate the mission and purpose to the community. Discover how your board can partner with organizational staff to implement mission and supporting policies.

Ingram, Richard T. *Ten Basic Responsibilities of Nonprofit Boards*. Washington, DC: Board-Source, 2003. More than 150,000 board members have already discovered this #1 BoardSource bestseller. This revised edition explores the 10 core areas of board responsibility. Share with board members the basic responsibilities, including determining mission and purpose, ensuring effective planning, and participating in fundraising. You'll find that this is an ideal reference for drafting job descriptions, assessing board performance, and orienting board members on their responsibilities.

Masaoka, Jan. *All Hands on Board: The Board of Directors in an All-Volunteer Organization* (E-Book). Washington, DC and San Francisco, CA: BoardSource and CompassPoint Nonprofit Services, 1999. Written for organizations without paid staff, this book describes the 10 jobs common to boards of all-volunteer organizations. It also includes a checklist measuring the board's level of job satisfaction.

Tesdahl, D. Benson. *The Nonprofit Board's Guide to Bylaws: Creating a Framework for Effective Governance*. Washington, DC: BoardSource, 2003. It is important that your board periodically review and adjust its bylaws in response to organizational change and growth. This revised book will help your board determine how your organization is best structured, the rights of the participants within the structure, and important organizational procedures. Included in the text are findings from a BoardSource conducted survey, providing recent empirical data about how nonprofits handle certain issues. Don't miss the sample bylaws provisions and the conflicts-of-interest policies on the accompanying CD-ROM!

ADOLESCENT

Axelrod, Nancy R. *Chief Executive Succession Planning: The Board's Role in Securing Your Organization's Future*. Washington, DC: BoardSource, 2002. Chief executive succession planning is not only about determining your organization's next leader. It is a continuous process that assesses your organization's needs and identifies leadership that supports those needs. A successful succession plan is linked to your organization's strategic plan, mission, and vision. Author Nancy Axelrod helps board members prepare for the future by examining the ongoing and intermittent steps of executive succession planning.

Berger, Steven. *Understanding Nonprofit Financial Statements*. Washington, DC: BoardSource, 2003. The newly revised and expanded edition of this bestselling title brings an understanding to key accounting terms and concepts, important benchmarking ratios, and sample nonprofit financial statements. Steven Berger's no-nonsense explanations are helpful for board members, treasurers, finance committee members, and staff who prepare financial information for the board.

Gale, Robert L. *Leadership Roles in Nonprofit Governance*. Washington, DC: BoardSource, 2003. Strong nonprofit board leadership is important to the success of your organization. This book clarifies the difference in the roles of the chief executive and board chair and provides suggestions for how this partnership can be strengthened. Discover how this leadership can effectively work with the governance committee to facilitate board development. Don't miss the sample job descriptions and a discussion on "What Keeps the President Awake at Night."

George, Worth. *Fearless Fundraising for Nonprofit Boards*. Washington, DC: BoardSource, 2003. Author Worth George has developed a system that will help disinclined board members get started on their fundraising responsibility. By providing specific choices and instructions, this resource helps to encourage once-reluctant board members to become active fundraisers. The book's centerpiece is a worksheet of 40 specific fundraising activities that range from simple to sophisticated, and all play an important part in the overall plan. With so many options to choose from, board members of every level of skill and experience can find a way to contribute to this critical role of fundraising.

Hopkins, Bruce R. *Legal Responsibilities of Nonprofit Boards*. Washington, DC: BoardSource, 2003. All board members should understand their legal responsibilities, including when and how they can be held personally liable and what type of oversight they should provide. Discover the essential information that board members should know to protect themselves and their organization. Written in non-technical language, this book provides legal concepts and definitions, as well as a detailed discussion on ethics.

Kocsis, Deborah L. and Susan A. Waechter. *Driving Strategic Planning: A Nonprofit Executive's Guide*. Washington, DC: BoardSource, 2003. This book will help the chief executive learn how to work with staff and board to assess the readiness of your organization and prepare for strategic planning. Discover a variety of approaches for dealing with common issues and overcoming organizational resistance to beginning the process. Review the fundamental elements of the strategic planning process, from mission and vision to environmental scan and competitive analysis.

Perrone, Michela M. and Janis Johnston. *Presenting: Strategic Planning. Choosing the Right Method for Your Nonprofit Organization*. Washington, DC: BoardSource 2005. Use this tool to promote the decision making needed to proceed with a strategic planning process. It includes a 30-page User's Guide and CD-ROM with PowerPoint presentations and electronic sample documents that are ready-made and customizable. The presentation is designed to provide an introduction to the strategic planning process, questions for assessing the organization's readiness to plan, a detailed outline of what board and staff should expect during planning, and a thorough step-by-step look at different approaches to planning so that board and staff can choose the right method for designing the organization's future.

MATURE

BoardSource. *The Source: Twelve Principles of Governance That Power Exceptional Boards*. Washington, DC: BoardSource 2005. Exceptional boards add significant value to their organizations, making discernible differences in their advance on mission. *The Source* defines governance not as dry, obligatory compliance, but as a creative and collaborative process that supports chief executives, engages board members, and furthers the causes they all serve. It enables nonprofit boards to operate at the highest and best use of their collective capacity. Aspirational in nature, these principles offer chief executives a description of an empowered board that is a strategic asset to be leveraged, and provide board members with a vision of what is possible and a way to add lasting value to the organizations they lead.

BoardSource Committee Series. Washington, DC: BoardSource, 2004. A panel of experts provides a fresh look at how board committees should be structured; they examine functional responsibilities, committee-to-board relationships, how to prepare for potential new legal regulations, and more. The series includes six individually-authored books on 1) transforming board structures, 2) governance committees, 3) executive committees, 4) financial committees, 5) development committees, and 6) advisory councils. Books can be purchased individually or as a set.

Chait, Richard P., William P. Ryan and Barbara E. Taylor. *Governance as Leadership: Reframing the Work of Nonprofit Boards*. New York: John Wiley & Sons and Washington, DC: BoardSource, 2005. *Governance as Leadership* introduces a fresh way to think about governance, with sensible guidance to turn these ideas into concrete actions. The book will be particularly valuable to staff of professionally managed nonprofit organizations, and to others, including foundation officers, donors, consultants, and students of nonprofit organizations, who are interested in improving nonprofit governance.

Hughes, Sandra R., Berit M. Lakey and Marla J. Bobowick. *The Board Building Cycle: Nine Steps to Finding, Recruiting, and Engaging Nonprofit Board Members*. Washington, DC: BoardSource, 2000. This book provides helpful tips on what motivates people to join boards, how and where to find board members, ideas for conducting an orientation session, and specific tasks for the board's governance committee. Also included are suggestions for involving former board members as advisors of committee members and removing difficult or ineffective board members. Included with *The Board Building Cycle* is a CD-ROM containing customizable worksheets and forms.

Mintz, Joshua and Jane Pierson. *Assessment of the Chief Executive: A Tool for Nonprofit Boards, Revised.* Washington, DC: BoardSource, 2005. By failing to adequately evaluate the chief executive, many nonprofit boards miss an opportunity to express support for the executive and strengthen his or her performance. This resource provides a comprehensive tool boards can use in the evaluation process. After discussing the benefits of assessment, the user's guide suggests a process and provides a questionnaire that addresses every major area of responsibility. Also included is a self-evaluation form for the executive to complete and share with the board. This resource is also available in a quick and easy-to-use online version. Contact BoardSource for more details.

Ober|Kaler, attorneys at law. *The Nonprofit Legal Landscape.* Washington, DC: BoardSource, 2005. Designed for executives and board members, *The Nonprofit Legal Landscape* explains the laws and legal concepts that affect nonprofit organizations. It serves as a handy reference tool for laws specific to tax exemption and for those regulating general business practices. When confronted with legal questions, nonprofit leaders can use this easy-to-read resource to rise rapidly to the next level of understanding.

Self-Assessment for Nonprofit Governing Boards. Washington, DC: BoardSource, 1999. BoardSource's proven assessment book is designed to help nonprofit boards determine how well they're carrying out their responsibilities and identify areas that need improvement. This evaluation toolkit includes a user's guide and 15 board member questionnaires so that you can easily distribute them to your board. This resource is also available in a quick and easy-to-use online version. Contact BoardSource for more details.

STAGNANT

Andringa, Robert C. and Ted W. Engstrom. *Nonprofit Board Answer Book: Practical Guidelines for Board Members and Chief Executives.* Washington, DC: BoardSource, 2001. BoardSource has created the next best thing to sitting down face to face with thousands of board members and chief executives! Our revised edition of the bestselling *Nonprofit Board Answer Book* is organized in an easy-to-follow question-and-answer format and covers almost every situation you're likely to encounter in nonprofit board governance, from structuring a board for success to nurturing strategic alliances with other organizations. Also included are action steps, real-life examples, and worksheets.

Andringa, Robert C. *Nonprofit Board Answer Book II: Beyond the Basics.* Washington, DC: BoardSource, 2002. Learn how to answer the hard questions posed by seasoned nonprofit executives who have moved beyond the basics of nonprofit management to confront the tougher issues. Building on the success of the *Nonprofit Board Answer Book,* this collection of questions and answers explores the governance successes of nonprofit organizations, detailed action steps, and provides the facts you need to move into such uncharted waters as launching a for-profit subsidiary, rebranding your organization, or surviving a merger. You'll learn how to effectively deal with thorny risk management, conflict of interest, and performance issues.

Flynn, Outi. *Meet Smarter: A Guide to Better Nonprofit Board Meetings.* Washington, DC: BoardSource, 2004. Whether you're new to the boardroom or an old pro, you'll find ready-to-use information in this resource. Based on actual meeting observations, this book will provide you with practical solutions to better meetings, explanation of the legal framework, and process practices that will reinvigorate your board meetings. With a detailed table of contents, this book is a must-have reference guide for nonprofit chief executives, board members, senior staff, and any other participant in key meetings of the board.

About the Author

Paul Connolly is senior vice president at TCC Group, a firm that provides management consulting, strategic planning, and evaluation services to nonprofit organizations, philanthropies, and government agencies (see www.tccgrp.com for more information about the firm). He leads the firm's philanthropy practice, previously oversaw the firm's nonprofit practice, and serves on the firm's board of directors. He is a consultant, manager, educator, and writer, and is especially knowledgeable about and experienced in organizational capacity building, strategic planning, grantmaking, evaluation, cultural participation, and social enterprise.

Mr. Connolly has provided consulting services to a wide array of nonprofit organizations, and has assisted a variety of funders to plan, implement, and evaluate capacity-building activities. He has been a presenter at national conferences, a trainer and facilitator for numerous regional grantmaker and nonprofit associations, and a lecturer at universities. He has served on the boards of a community health center, a local community board, and an artist's credit union. He is co-author of *Strengthening Nonprofit Performance: A Funder's Guide to Capacity Building* (with Carol Lukas) and *Increasing Cultural Participation: An Audience Development Handbook for Presenters, Producers, and Their Collaborators* (with Marcelle Hinand Cady).

Before joining TCC Group nine years ago, Mr. Connolly was associate director of Nonprofit Facilities Fund (NFF), where he oversaw operations and managed consulting, training, and publishing services. Previously, he was a management consultant for nonprofit organizations, working independently in New York and at Storey and Green Associates in San Francisco. Earlier in his career, he worked in New York City government and at Pfizer Inc.'s Public Affairs Division, a Regional Development Authority in the Netherlands, and the U.K. Inner Cities Directorate.

Mr. Connolly received his master's degree in Public and Private Management from Yale School of Management, where he was awarded the Jess Morrow Johns Memorial Scholarship, and a bachelor of arts degree with honors from Harvard University.

Paul Connolly can be reached at TCC Group, 50 E. 42nd Street, 19th Floor, NY, NY 10017; 212-949-0990, extension 218; pconnolly@tccgrp.com.